KEYS TO PARENTING YOUR FOUR YEAR OLD

Meri Wallace, M.S.W.

D0877345

BARRON'S

Cover Photo © 1997 Photodisc, Inc.

Dedication
To my loving husband, Jonathan, for his tremendous support and assistance on this project and in my life; my devoted son, Michael, and daughter-in-law, Meredith, for enriching my life and giving me much joy as a parent; my mother, Niravi, for all her support and encouragement to follow my dreams; and my father, Albert, and stepmother, Arlene, for all their love.

© Copyright 1997 by Barron's Educational Series, Inc.

All rights reserved.
No part of this book may be reproduced in any form, by photostat, microfilm, xerography, or any other means, or incorporated into any information retrieval system, electronic or mechanical, without the written permission of the copyright owner.

All inquiries should be addressed to:
Barron's Educational Series, Inc.
250 Wireless Boulevard
Hauppauge, New York 11788

Library of Congress Catalog Card No. 97-6351

International Standard Book No. 0-8120-9745-9

Library of Congress Cataloging-in-Publication Data
Wallace, Meri.
    Keys to parenting your four year old / Meri Wallace.
        p.   cm. — (Barron's parenting keys)
    Includes index.
    ISBN 0-8120-9745-9
    1. Child rearing. 2. Parenting. I. Title. II. Series.
HQ769.W193   1997
649′ .1—dc21   97-6351
                                                              CIP

PRINTED IN THE UNITED STATES OF AMERICA
98765432

CONTENTS

INTRODUCTION

A PORTRAIT OF YOUR FOUR YEAR OLD

Heather lifts herself carefully to the top of the monkey bars. She stretches her arm out to the side and bursts into a song. "A Whole New World," she sings (the theme song from *Aladdin*), and gestures as if she is a well-known star of stage and screen and the world is her audience. She is singing from the bottom of her soul and is unconcerned that no one is listening.

At this moment, Heather embodies the very essence of every four year old. She is in love with the world, with you, her friends, and herself!

As children grow, they grasp more and more about life and themselves each year. At four, it is as if their eyes open wide for the first time, and they are dizzy with excitement. They feel strong and bring an almost unbridled life force to whatever they do. They want to see and experience everything.

This year will be an exciting one for you and your child as her abilities blossom in every sphere of life.

At this age, you may find that she can dress herself, make a colorful birthday card for you, and chat about her new dress with anyone she meets. Though she loves to be on the move, running and skipping or riding on her new RollerBlades, she will probably enjoy sitting and looking at a book for longer periods than she did a year ago.

You will be surprised by her use of language ("Actually, I would rather have carrots"), her new social finesse ("Let's share the shovel"), and how much she looks like a miniature adult in her jeans. Her ability to absorb countless new facts and her inquisitiveness about birth, death, and other complex concepts will simply astound you. You may also find that this year, you can reason with her and talk through problems more successfully.

As marvelous as she is, she may be a handful at times, too. Four year olds can be very argumentative, bossy, and noncompliant as they attempt to assert their independence. "You aren't the boss of me," is often heard by parents. Your child will also be very demanding. She may alternate between insisting that you dress her and refusing to wear anything you choose. She will probably have strong preferences about how she wears her hair, what she eats for dinner, and which side of the street she walks on.

This year, her mood swings will be intense. She will declare her love for you one moment, only to scream "I hate you!" seconds later if you disappoint her.

Although her impulse control is growing, if you accidentally allow her mashed potatoes to touch her peas, or say no to a play date with her best friend, she may still spin out of control. She may call you and your relatives "pee-pee head," or kick her brother.

Some of your four year old's greatest developmental challenges this year will be to become more independent, to learn to control her aggression and other impulses, to manage her feelings in more appropriate ways (e.g., to say "I'm mad" instead of hitting), and to learn how to cope with more complicated peer relationships.

As she faces these challenges, she will need your love and emotional support. You must be a patient, respectful educator who teaches her coping skills, shares in her excitement for life, and, above all, gives her a positive feeling about herself and her natural development. This book will help you accomplish these important goals.

Keys to Parenting Your Four Year Old celebrates the joy and exuberance of this stage of your child's development. It provides you with insight into your child's emotional world and behavior while offering you valuable phrases and management techniques to help you respond effectively. The goal of this book is to enrich the experience of your child's fourth year of life for both you and your child.

Part one explores some general trends in a four year old's development. (In each chapter, I alternate between the pronouns *he* and *she* to make the book more personal and cohesive.)

This information is crucial for parents as they try to figure out their child's behaviors (e.g., why she is taking candy from a grocery shelf or is refusing to clean her room). Parents often jump to conclusions and assign adult meanings to a child's behavior (e.g., "Oh no—she is going to be a thief," or "She is going to be a slob").

Knowing that it is natural for four year olds to take things because they are governed by their impulses, and that the child will cease such behavior as you set limits and she gains better control around five, helps reduce the parents' anxiety. (There is nothing wrong with the child or your parenting skills!)

Knowing that most four year olds would rather play than clean up enables parents to readjust their expectations (it is natural for her to resist), to communicate more effectively ("Let's do it together"), and to avoid using labels (*messy* or *lazy*) that undermine a child's self-esteem.

As you read Part One, keep in mind that each aspect of development is a process (e.g., the ability to write one's name or participate in a group) and that each child has her own particular growth pattern. (Some children walk by nine months while others are beginning to use words at this age.) If you detect a lag in your child's development, however, trust your gut reaction and consult with your pediatrician.

There is no one ideal mold for a four year old. Thank goodness! For in time, before your very eyes, your child's own unique personality and plentiful talents will unfold.

Part Two focuses on how you can foster your child's independence, self-esteem, and emotional, cognitive, and social development.

Part Three examines some specific challenges, such as how to explain birth and cope with sibling rivalry. You will obtain an understanding of the issues and effective techniques to help you respond.

Part Four concentrates on how to help your child behave appropriately and get along with others. It provides you with positive phrases that you can use to communicate successfully with your child.

Part Five explores the value of play and the preschool experience and how children's learning skills evolve.

The material in this book is drawn from my 23 years of motherhood and from my 15 years of professional experience as a psychotherapist treating adults, children, couples, and families; a parent educator; and a consultant to nursery schools. I hope my ideas will help you to enjoy parenting your child and, in particular, this phase of your child's development. Above all, enjoy this wondrous stage fully! It is fleeting.

Acknowledgments

Special thanks to Nina Calaman for her superb work; Linda Turner, my editor, for her excellent guidance and support; Lydia Weaver for teaching me all about writing; my nieces and nephews and my friends for their invaluable support; Madeleine Calaman, Amy and Liliana Silverman, Cindy Harden and Christopher Bussolini, Donna and Michael Gordon, Magna Antoine, Eileen Shannon, all the members of my parent support groups, and the staff and children at Open House Nursery School.

1

GROSS MOTOR DEVELOPMENT

Michael swings on a tire with his friend David. Then he races across the yard, climbs up on the jungle gym, swings from a bar, and jumps down to the ground. Next, he throws a ball in the air and runs after it.

Your four year old loves movement. If he seems like a perpetual-motion machine at times, don't worry—it's just his natural development. Your child likes to run, leap, jump, whirl, and do somersaults. He brings a zest for life and tons of energy to his activity. This year, your child will have wonderful new abilities. (Keep in mind that children vary tremendously in their growth patterns. If your child is not yet doing some of the activities described here, he will soon be able to do them.)

Having lost his toddleresque potbelly, your child is leaner and more agile, so he moves more gracefully through space. Your child walks with long swinging steps and looks like a little adult. He may walk adeptly across the top of a low, narrow wall like a tightrope walker, without holding on to your hand, because his balance is more highly developed. (He can also stand on one foot for four to eight seconds, hop several times in a row, jump down from a height of two feet or more, and land with both feet together.)

1

Your four year old may sit on a swing and pump until he is high in the air (although he might ask you for a few pushes to get started). He is speedy and maneuvers with ease around all obstacles when he runs, skips (one foot at a time this year), or gallops. If he falls, which happens less often than it used to, he quickly picks himself up and keeps going. He will come to you less for consolation this year, but he will still cry and need your comfort when he is hurt.

Your child can throw a ball overhand with better aim than when he was younger and will try to catch it with his hands rather than his arms. Don't expect him to be able to catch it successfully for at least another year or two, however.

By now, he may easily climb up a ladder, the monkey bars, and even the front of a slide, so you will be able to stand back and worry less that he will fall. Your child can hold on to a bannister and walk upstairs one foot at a time. (The way down might be a little harder.)

This year, your four year old's coordination is better and he has developed an inner awareness of what he can do with his body. These abilities give him greater control over his activities, so that he can participate more successfully in movement games such as "Simon Says," dance classes, and sports. He may also be able to roller-skate, ride a bike with training wheels, or even ride a two-wheeler.

Your four year old is daring and loves new challenges. If he was afraid to come down the slide on his stomach last year, he will gleefully try it over and over again this year until he masters it. He feels great pride when he does accomplish a new feat (much the way an adult feels when he's perfected a new tennis stroke). His cries of "Daddy, look at me" or "Mommy, watch me" will ring out throughout the day, and he will need you to respond: "Wow! That's great!" or "I like the way you did that" to his tiniest achievement. You will also have to supervise him, even from afar, so that you can prevent him from doing something that's too dangerous, such as sitting on top of the jungle gym without holding on.

Your child may want you to help him with a new trick—for example, by keeping your hands by his waist as he walks hand over hand across the monkey bars, letting him hold your finger as he walks across a high wall, or helping him on to a pole so that he can slide down (until he feels more confident). Try not to move in too quickly, though. Wait to see if he asks you for help—he may be able to see it through on his own, or with some words of encouragement. Avoid criticizing him, even if he's not doing something perfectly; otherwise, he might stop trying.

Your child may sometimes enjoy moving from one activity to another, whereas at other times he can play one game for a long time. Some parents worry that their active child might be hyperactive. If he can focus on one activity, such as building with Bristle Blocks, for approximately 15 to 20 minutes, he is probably just a normal, active four year old. Sometimes children can be overactive if they are tired, anxious, angry, or in need of attention. (For further discussion, see question on Attention Deficit Hyperactivity Disorder in Questions and Answers.)

Your child's high energy level and constant need for physical activity can create special challenges for you as you go through your daily routine. It is important to convey to your child that you accept his need to move (so that he will continue to feel good about physical expression), give him ample opportunities for activity, and provide him with appropriate boundaries to ensure his safety. (See Key 18 on safety.)

If you've been waiting in a long line, sitting in a doctor's office for hours, or shopping in one store after another, your child may start running around, hiding in between the clothes, or rolling on the floor. Avoid saying, "What's the matter with you? You're so wild!" (This could cause your child to feel ashamed of his natural need to move.) Instead, tell him that you know it is hard for a child his age to be still so long, and offer him a book, a healthy snack, or a game to keep him occupied. When you are finished, take a trip to the park.

On a long car trip, stop every so often to let your child walk around. When you are stuck indoors on a rainy day and he is getting cranky and overly active, put on a children's exercise tape, or give him a mat or some pillows so that he can practice his karate moves and somersaults.

This is a great age at which to enroll your child in a creative movement program or in swimming, gymnastics, or karate classes, where he can use his new body awareness to develop his motor skills. These programs should be fun for your child, expand his abilities, and build his self-confidence. Their purpose is not primarily to produce stars. Try not to criticize the way your child moves or pressure him to perform, or he might withdraw from an activity.

If you had aspirations to become a ballerina or a major league baseball player when you were young and your child just isn't interested, try not to become overinvested. He might not like baseball this year but he may be drawn to it in a few years, or he might find that swimming is the love of his life. Try to help him to cultivate his own interests while exposing him to new activities from time to time.

If you accept your child's exuberance, give him some independence and admiration, and provide him with plenty of outlets for his energy, your child will grow up feeling free to enjoy physical activity. If you are tired out by racing after him to get dressed in the morning or by keeping up with him at the park, be patient; by the age of five, he may be less active and might enjoy looking at books or doing art projects for hours.

2

FINE MOTOR DEVELOPMENT

Meredith places her hand on the paper and carefully makes an outline with a fine marker. She glues a small black circle near the top of the thumb, representing an eye. Next, she makes intricate colored designs on the four fingers and finishes by pasting small feathers all over the hand and drawing two feet. She writes her name at the bottom of the paper and holds her picture up to her friend. "Look, I made a hand turkey," she announces.

As you watch your child playing, you will marvel at the more skillful and creative tasks she can perform. This year, your child's fine motor skills are just blossoming!

At three, your child may have drawn or painted a person by making a circle, two eyes, a nose, and a mouth, and perhaps she added two lines for arms and two lines for legs extending from the head. Many four year olds now add an oval or a square for the body and more details, such as hair, eyebrows, ears, a neck, and even a belly button. Last year, your child would color in areas with lines and patches of color and say, "It's a playground"; this year, your child may surprise you in her drawings and paintings with her attempts at representational objects, such as a tree, a flower, or a cat. (See Figure 1.)

Liliana Silverman

Your child will demonstrate her fine motor prowess as she manipulates her toys more skillfully than she could at three years old. She may be able to string tiny beads and even copy a pattern. She can fit together the tracks for her new train set or close the snaps on her doll's new dress.

This year, she will assemble more intricate constructions with Legos, Duplos, Tinkertoys, mini waffle blocks, and Bristle Blocks. Her refined stacking abilities will enable her to build larger, more elaborate wooden block structures.

At four, your child may like to work with clay. She can roll the clay with her hands, flatten it with a rolling pin, and make varied shapes with a cookie cutter. Her clay work will also become more representational this year. She might make you or her friend a pie, or she might point to her flat, green piece of clay with little round balls on it and say, "This is a pond with ducks."

This year, with improved hand-eye coordination, your child has greater facility with puzzles (even those with 24 pieces or more). She may be able to follow mazes in a book, complete connect-the-dot pictures, and color within the lines in a coloring book. Coloring books can help build your child's fine motor skills but should not be the only drawing experience your child has. She needs the opportunity to color freely and use her own ideas.

Drawing is an important activity for your child as she enters a great phase of creativity this year, and it may be one of her favorite pastimes (although many children prefer other forms of self-expression). As she draws, she learns how to control lines and shapes (prerequisites for writing), she deepens her understanding of the world (she knows her flower needs a stem, petals, leaves, and roots), and she can express her own ideas and feelings (she can draw a sad purple tree). Be sure to provide her with ample materials (paper,

7

crayons, markers, pens, and pencils) and praise, and avoid correcting her (even if her cat doesn't look like one). Thick markers and crayons are easier to grasp and will facilitate this activity for some children.

Your child may hold her marker, crayon, or pencil between her thumb and forefinger this year like an adult (if not this year, she will by age six), and this grasp will aid her attempts to write. Some children start writing at four, whereas others are not interested until the following year. (See Key on reading, writing, and math skills, to learn about the development of these skills.)

This is the year when many children begin making art projects. Your four year old may be able to sit down and make greeting cards, paper dolls, or collages all by herself. She will set out with an idea and work hard, with greater concentration than when she was younger, until she is finished. (Provide her with lots of odds and ends—glitter, feathers, cut-up pieces of wool, or doilies—and she will put them to good use.)

If you are sitting with your child and she is having difficulty with a task, wait to see if she will ask for your help. Resolving problems is part of making a project. Above all, let your child direct her activity.

Your child's skills in using a stapler, glue, cellophane tape, and scissors (a small pair of safety scissors is best) are improving. She may be able to cut along a straight line and even cut out pictures for pasting. To sharpen these visual motor skills, have her help you with projects such as gift wrapping presents or cutting out coupons. Other activities that build fine motor skills include tracing (outlining shapes and letters with fat markers) and cooking (using an egg-beater, pouring liquids, or kneading dough).

When your child has made something out of clay, a drawing, a painting, or even a Lego construction, she is being creative. She is exploring different materials and using them to express her own unique view of the world. When she says, "Look what I made" (as she often will throughout the day), be careful not to rush in and say, "What a beautiful tree that is!" even if you are certain that this is what it is. Your child may be insulted if it was meant to be a scarecrow.

Avoid criticizing her work—for example, picking up a pencil or reassembling her Legos and saying, "This is the way a scarecrow really looks." (Her creation is part of herself. If it's not good in your eyes, she might think that she's not good.) It would be sad to see your child decide at age four that she does not know how to draw or to build with Legos.

Instead, when she shows you her creation, say, "Tell me about it." If you find yourself repeating "That's great" and are looking for a way to respond differently, you can relate to a part of her work. You can say, "I like the way those lines curve" or "I like the colors of the sky" and find some way to put her work on display—if she would like that, of course.

This year, your child's improved finger dexterity will help with her self-care. She may brush her teeth better, comb her hair, button her shirt, zip her jacket, untie her laces, and even make an attempt to tie them. She might be able to use a knife to butter her pancakes or even twirl spaghetti on her fork. Be careful not to criticize her attempts at new tasks; otherwise, she will be afraid to try. Instead, work patiently with her and show her how.

Hammering a nail or using a screwdriver is exciting to a four year old, but she must be carefully supervised. She may be able to open jars and tightly wrapped packages and even pick up small objects with tweezers. This year, your child can also correctly operate more complicated machines, such as a tape recorder, a television, a radio, an electric mixer, and even a computer.

If you allow your child to experiment creatively, praise her for her attempts, and provide her with materials, your child's fine motor skills will continue to develop, and before you know it, she will be tying her shoes, writing stories, and even playing tunes on the piano.

3

LANGUAGE DEVELOPMENT

Four-year-old Jonathan tells his friend a joke:
"Knock, knock."
"Who's there?"
"Banana."
"Banana who?"
"Banana pajama!"

If you are talking to your child and you forget that he is only four years old, that's probably because he is so verbal! Your child loves to talk, whisper, sing, and shout. He is very social and will share information about himself with just about anyone he meets. He will tell your neighbor, "My Mom has a new dress," or a child at the park, "I have a fire truck at home." (He speaks clearly in a more adult voice this year, so you won't have to translate for him as much as in the past.) He will talk to his stuffed rabbit and even to himself when he is playing alone. Some parents say that the only time their four year old is quiet is when he is sound asleep. (Remember, just as four year olds differ in their physical growth, so, too, do their language abilities, such as pronunciation, sentence formation, and word usage, vary.)

Your child's language is rich and colorful. He enjoys playing with words through rhymes ("I'm going to get my hat in my cat, on the mat"), exaggerations ("I love you more than a million stars"), and downright silliness ("I went to the zoo and saw a chicken monkey and a chicken gorilla") to make you laugh. Sometimes his wordplay, silliness, and exaggeration with words can get him into trouble. (See Key 17 on name-calling.)

Expressive Language (Speaking)

This year, your child uses language in more sophisticated ways. He can state his needs more clearly ("Please close the blinds; the sun is in my eyes"), question you in a more grown-up fashion ("Mommy, what TV programs did you watch when you were small?"), and express his emotions in words ("You're hurting my feelings"). He uses language to negotiate with his peers ("It's my turn now; it will be your turn next "), to assert himself ("Stop hitting me"), or to carry out pretend play ("Good-bye. I have to go to work right now").

At four, his vocabulary is exploding (more than 1,500 words) and he speaks in sentences of more than five words. He may surprise you by his eloquent use of complex sentences, such as "Actually, I have decided that I would rather walk to school today than take the bus."

His sentence structure and grammatical usage are more accurate. He adds an *s* to verbs in the present tense (she *walks*, he *runs*) and can express possession properly (*your* book becomes *yours*). He will still make noticeable mistakes this year, however. For example, he might *say* foots or *mices* because he's learned from listening that to make a plural noun, you add an *s*, or *builded* because to form the past tense, you add *ed*. Until he learns irregular nouns and verbs, he will use these forms.

This year, he is working on the pronunciation of the more difficult speech sounds *l*, *r*, *s*, *t*, *sh*, *ch*, *j*, and *th*. He may not fully master them, however, until he is six or seven.

Psgehhti

When your child mispronounces a word, such as baf for bath, or uses the wrong tense of a verb, such as builded for built, do not correct him, tease him, or punish him (he is not doing this on purpose). It is better to repeat what he was trying to express, correctly, in a natural voice and context. For example: "Yes, it's time for your bath," or "The airplane you built with Dad is beautiful." Your child is a great learner, and as he listens to you and uses language over time, he will correct himself.

Stuttering (Speech Disfluency)

It is natural for four year olds to stutter at times (hesitate when they speak, or repeat a phrase, a whole word, or part of a word several times). This occurs when the child's thoughts go quicker than his words, especially when he is excited or anxious. If he stutters, avoid saying, "You're stuttering," "Start over," or "Speak slowly," and do not jump in to finish his words.

Instead, speak to your child at a slow, relaxed speed (as a model for him); use your facial expressions and other body language to convey that you are listening to the content of his speech and not to how he is talking; and try to avoid situations that seem to evoke this response, such as pressuring him to tell your relatives about school.

Sometimes a child's stuttering is related to an emotional issue. If your child began stuttering during some family upheaval (e.g., a divorce or the birth of a sibling) or stutters only under certain duress (e.g., when he is criticized), he is probably having an emotional reaction. He might be afraid to express his true feelings. In this case, make sure to listen noncritically when he speaks, do not interrupt him, and encourage him to express his feelings (especially his anger), and the stuttering should gradually decrease.

Receptive Language (Understanding)

Your four year old can comprehend your requests and follow your directions (even three in a row). For example, he will understand "Pick up your plate, clean it off in the garbage, and put it in the sink." He can listen to a story, absorb the meaning, and talk to you about what is happening (keeping to the story line).

If your child does not seem to understand you and it is clear that it is not natural resistance, he may have a hearing problem (frequent earaches can affect a child's hearing and speech) or difficulty in processing language (interpreting what he hears).

When to Get Help

Your child should have speech and hearing evaluations by a speech and language pathologist for any of the following symptoms: He mispronounces many words, he is very difficult to understand (most four year olds should be understood even by nonfamily members by now), he does not seem to comprehend what is said, or he stutters frequently or for a duration of two to three months or shows signs of duress (e.g., facial tics) when he tries to express himself. Keep in mind that delayed speech does not mean that your child is not smart; nor does it reflect negatively upon his worth or your own.

Though it may be difficult for you to acknowledge that there might be a problem (you love your child and want him to be trouble-free), it is crucial that he get help. With the proper treatment, he can overcome his difficulties. Otherwise, if he cannot communicate with others, he will grow up feeling socially isolated.

If your child needs speech therapy, do not worry. At this age, speech therapy is often done through play in a relaxed setting. You can ask your child's doctor for a referral to a

competent speech therapist or to a mental health professional (if it is determined that your child's problem may be
emotional). For other referral sources, consult the resource
list at the back of this book.

Encouraging Language Development

The best way for your child to develop his language
skills is for him to talk to you. When he does, your child
should get the message that what he has to say is important.

Spend time talking alone with your child each day, giving him your undivided attention (you can set aside at least
15 minutes). Be sure to turn off all background noise, especially the TV, so that you can hear each other clearly. Let him
tell you what he has been thinking, doing, and feeling. Ask
him, "Did you paint at school?" or "What did Taiwan do to
make you mad?" (Specific questions are easier to answer
than general questions, e.g., "What did you do today?" He did
so many things that he may not know what to say.) If he does
not say too much, listen to him throughout the day, and
when he announces "Amanda fell down at school," you have
an opening for a conversation.

Be a good listener. Give your child direct eye contact (it
shows you are interested) and time to formulate his
thoughts, and don't interrupt him. Respond nonverbally
while listening (you can nod your head), or say, "Tell me
more," "What happened after that?" or "You must have been
angry" to stimulate more discussion.

During a family discussion, encourage everyone to
make room for your child to speak, and validate his ideas (a
child needs to be seen *and* heard). If he is speaking nonstop,
avoid saying, "Can't you ever stop talking?" or calling him a
chatterbox (he will feel guilty for speaking and may withdraw). Instead, tell him, "Now it's time for your sister to
speak. We want to hear what you have to say, but you need

to sit quietly for a few minutes." This approach teaches him to be a good listener.

Reading to your child is also very important. As he listens to the words and expresses his ideas about the story, he will enhance his pronunciation, word usage, vocabulary, and comprehension. You can ask him, "Which part of the story did you like?" or "Why do you think the bunny ran away?"

Always model good communication skills for your child. It is primarily from you that he will learn how to speak with others.

If you talk to your child, listen to what he has to say, and create a calm atmosphere where all his thoughts and feelings are acceptable, your child will feel free to express himself verbally as he goes through life.

4

COGNITIVE DEVELOPMENT

W hen your child was only two months old, she would lie in her carriage staring at some leaves at the top of a tree. As she gazed steadfastly, you may have wondered, "What is she looking at so intently? Is she studying the shape of the leaves, how they move in the breeze, or the way the light plays upon them?" One thing was certain— she was busy discovering!

At four, your child has the same innate zest to learn. She loves new ideas, challenges, and problem solving. As her parent, you have the joy of experiencing the world anew through her eyes and watching her mind expand.

Every day, your child gathers information through her play; at school; from television, movies, and books; and from observing others. She will also question you with her incessant "whys?" Her curiosity brings her to ask, "Why is there a rainbow in the sky? Why couldn't Cinderella go to the ball?"

Your child needs you to be her partner in learning. When she questions you, try to demonstrate an openness to talk about any topic, and convey to her that all her ideas are valuable. (Do not hesitate to say, "I have to think about this," "I really do not know," or "Let's look this up when we get home" when you are unsure of how to answer.)

As you discuss issues with her, you must keep in mind that she does not understand the world in the same way that a mature adult does. She lacks the perspective gained from years of life experience that you have, as well as the ability to process information that is too abstract, so you will need to adjust your explanations.

How Your Child Thinks

At four, your child is a concrete thinker. She comprehends more easily what she has experienced firsthand, and she learns best through her senses. If you want to acquaint her with the color turquoise, it is best to show her a patch of the color in a rug. If you say, "It is like blue," she will not visualize it as well.

Whenever you explain an abstract concept, she will need you to break it down into simpler parts and liken it to her own experience. For example, if she asks you what *freedom* means, you can say, "You know how in our house we each have the chance to say how we feel about things? That is freedom."

Your child is a magical thinker. Just as when she was a baby, she thought her crying produced milk, she still thinks her actions, wishes, thoughts, and feelings can cause events to happen. A sick child will say, "If I drink all my juice, I'll be better," or an angry child might threaten, "I will make you disappear." If you have an argument right before you are going away on a long trip, your child might conclude that you are leaving because you are angry with her. (Reassure her that this is not the case!) As adults, we still can be magical thinkers from time to time.

The four year old is still an egocentric thinker. She experiences herself as the center of the universe and sees the world from her own point of view. When you are lying on the couch ill and cannot play with her, she will be more concerned with your lack of availability to her than with your discomfort. It is not that she is selfish. This year, she is only beginning to conceptualize how an experience would feel to the other person. (See discussion of empathy in Key on emotional development.)

Your child is a literal thinker. If you say, "I was so scared that my heart skipped a beat" (a heart can skip?) or "Time flies when you are having fun," (time can fly?), she may look at you with astonished eyes, so you will need to explain. Tell her it is a "figure of speech" and she will enjoy recognizing new ones in conversations.

This year, she is working hard on the notions of "real" and "pretend." Intellectually, she knows that nightmares and bad people on television are not real, but she will still need your assurance. She will often say, "Is that pretend?" when a character gets killed in a movie. Be aware that she may become panicked by your offhanded statements, such as "I passed that stop sign. That policeman is going to kill us!"

What Your Child Knows

By four, your child has developed astounding cognitive abilities. She is learning to link specific information into patterns or concepts (e.g., balls, oranges, and pennies are round; a dog, a giraffe, and a buffalo are animals) and comprehends that a word, picture, or mental image (symbols) can stand for the real object (she can draw a picture of her house). These achievements will help her to become an abstract thinker over time.

Children's learning skills vary greatly. Do not worry if your child's friend can count higher, or if your child would rather draw flowers than write her name. By the end of the first grade, she will be reading, writing, and doing math. Be sure to praise (and never criticize) your child's attempts. She will try more and will feel like a competent learner.

When you point out shapes as you walk along, she will recognize the most common ones: circle, oval, square, rectangle, triangle, diamond, star, or heart. She may be able to match all the shapes in a ten-hole form board.

Your child can compare the sizes of things. If you ask her, she can tell you which person in a picture is larger, can state which clay worm is the longest of three, and may even be able to arrange five blocks from heaviest to lightest. She will still watch, however, as you pour the same quantity of water into a low, wide container and a tall, thin one, and decide that the tall one has more water. In her mind, she is also convinced that someone who is bigger is older.

When her friend asks for a crayon, she will be able to identify the colors red, yellow, green, blue, black, white, brown, orange, pink, and purple. At this age, your child may have a favorite color (e.g., she might want to wear purple all the way from her shirt down to her shoelaces).

Four year olds can generally count from 1 to 10, though many can count to 20 or higher. As your child practices, she will frequently mix up the order of numbers or get stuck, and so she may need your help. Do not be alarmed. By the age of five, she may flawlessly count up to 100, once she catches on to the concept of counting.

Most four year olds know a one-to-one correspondence between numbers and objects. When counting pennies in her piggybank, your child may be able to answer the questions, "What number comes after 3?" or "What happens if we take one penny away?"

At this age, your child's memory is very sharp. She may even remember what color Clarence the cat was in a story you read several weeks earlier. By now, she will probably know her first, middle, and last names; the name of her street; the city she lives in; and her birthday.

Four year olds understand the concepts past, present, and future. Your child will talk about "when I will be a mommy" or "when I was a teeny baby." In her daily language, she will use sophisticated phrases—such as "once a day," "usually," "meantime," "wintertime," "last summer," "in five minutes," and "next week"—that show she has a sense of the passage of time.

However, she is not able to grasp just how long a duration of time really is. When she speaks about past events, three days ago, or several weeks ago, she may say, "Yesterday we went to the zoo" or "The day before today we ate ice cream." She may also need you to remind her what comes next—for example, "After dinner, it is time for your bath."

You can help her by showing time measurements visually. For example, when you are going to the circus on Wednesday, in six days, mark off the days on a calendar or make a paper chain and remove one link for each day. She will have a clearer sense of when she will be going.

This year, your child perceives spatial relationships better. She can locate her doll on, under, in back of, beside, or in front of the couch and is familiar with other concepts, such as "far away" and "way up."

Children differ in their reading and writing abilities. Many four year olds can identify capital letters or at least the first letter of their name. Others know all the capital letters, can write their names, can identify lowercase letters, and recognize common street signs. (Always follow your child's lead and avoid rushing her in this area. See Key 35 on writing, reading, and math skills, for more information.)

This year, your child will greatly expand her knowledge and comprehension of the world. If you praise her achievements, validate her ideas, and help her in a noncritical, unpressured way, you will nurture her joy of learning.

5

EMOTIONAL DEVELOPMENT

Do you remember when your child was a tiny baby? When he was hungry, wet, or having gas pains, he cried. While you were getting ready to feed him, he would grow frantic and thrash around with his arms and legs. His needs seemed urgent to him, as if he would disintegrate if he had to wait. He was the center of his universe, reacting to his own internal sensations.

Now here he is, only a few years later, attached to the people in his environment, trusting that you will provide for him, and capable of expressing his needs. Your love and care have helped him to make enormous emotional strides.

Love and Independence

Each time your baby cried, you responded, and slowly but surely he began to recognize you and smiled whenever you approached. As you fed him, sang to him, and soothed his pain, he learned from you how to love another human being. When you kissed and hugged him and told him "I love you," he learned how to express his affection.

Now, at four, he loves you passionately. He adores his family, the babysitter, all the people in his immediate world. He will even tell you, "I love you around the world and back again" amid hugs and kisses. He has already taken his ability to love outside his home and formed warm, affectionate relationships with his relatives, teachers, and peers.

At the same time that he enjoys his closeness with you, he feels an urgent developmental need to become independent, establish his own identity, and gain some control. This year will be a turbulent one as he battles hard with you to assert himself. He will oppose your requests ("No! I won't get dressed"), ignore the rules (sneak an extra piece of candy), insist he is right, ("It is *not* cold"), and try to prove he is the boss ("I'm in charge"). He will also make your head spin as he alternates between insisting you feed him and pushing you away.

Around the age of five, he will begin to settle down as he feels more independent and confident in his new abilities. In the meantime, if you acknowledge his separateness, respect his feelings, offer him choices, and negotiate settlements, you will foster his independence and he will fight you less.

Trust and Delayed Gratification

As you fulfilled your child's needs, he learned that he could depend upon you. If you could not get to him right away, you called to him, "I will be there in a minute," and because of your reliable track record, he slowly learned how to put off immediate gratification and to tolerate some frustration.

At four, although he has a greater ability to wait than at age three, his needs still feel very urgent at times, so his reactions will vary. Sometimes when you tell him that you will help him with his sock after you finish brushing your teeth, he will be able to wait patiently. At other times, he may immediately start screaming, "You have to put it on right now!" and dissolve into tears.

You can help him build his tolerance for frustration in the following ways. When you say no to his request for a cookie before dinner, give him a reasonable explanation ("You will not have room for your meal"), offer him an alternative ("You can have a piece of carrot while you are waiting"), and negotiate a solution ("You can have a cookie after dinner"). Provide him with constant support, too. Tell him, "I know it is hard to wait," and be patient. He is new at this!

Empathy

When your child fell in the park, had a fever, or was disappointed about not getting a new toy, you may have scooped him up, kissed him, and soothed him with words. As you gave him that daily support, he learned how to be concerned about another person's feelings.

At four, he will ask you, "Do you feel better, Mommy?" when he knows you are sick or will kiss you on the forehead while you are recuperating in bed. Though his intentions are good, it will be hard for him to focus on your needs (at four, he is still egocentric; i.e., his needs and desires are the center of his universe). Do not be surprised when he jumps on the bed only a few minutes later or does not respond to "Mommy is sick, so you have to be quiet." (He may also act up when you are ill because he fears you will die and he will be all alone.)

As he grows, he will acknowledge your needs better and will extend the empathy he learns at home to a child who falls at the park or to an adult who is crying.

Sharing Attention and Jealousy

Infants need to be the center of attention, so that they can survive. That is why they are so demanding (probably this has an evolutionary derivation). Parents must make their baby a priority because he is so helpless. This attention makes the child feel safe and cared for.

At four, even though he needs your attention much less (he is more independent and can occupy himself for longer periods), your child still feels a powerful need for you and finds it almost impossible to tolerate your other activities at times (e.g., when you are cooking dinner, talking on the phone, or discussing a problem with your spouse). He wants to be your main focus.

Sharing your love and attention with a sibling, or even your spouse, can be extremely difficult for him. He may become intensely jealous and engage in negative, attention-seeking behaviors. It is important to accept his jealousy as a natural part of being a child. Tell him that you understand that it is hard for him to share your attention; if he feels angry, he can tell you, but he cannot hit you. Assure him that you have enough love for him, his sister, and your husband. (For ideas on helping your child cope with a sibling, see Key on sibling rivalry.) He will gain the ability to share you more easily, as he gets older.

In the meantime, most parents find that postponing telephone calls and other long adult conversations until after the child is asleep works best (you can use an answering machine during the evening routine). If you must be busy, tell him, "I know it is hard for you when I talk on the phone, but I need to right now." (Keep a special box with "telephone-time toys" on hand.)

If you have been away, work long hours, or have been focused on his sister's school play, plan some special individual time with your child.

Happiness and Sadness

In general, most four year olds feel happy and have a sense of well-being. They love their family, trust that their needs will be met, have a growing sense of independence, and can do more exciting things. They may even get giddy or silly from joy. It is important to accept your child's expression of happiness (even if he gets a little out of hand). Otherwise, he will become ashamed of his good feelings. You can always set a limit when you need to. Tell him, "It is wonderful that you are having fun, but if you need to be loud, please play in your room with your friend."

Your child's moods can shift dramatically this year because he experiences his emotions intensely. If a friend tells him, "I don't like you," your four year old may feel crushed and burst into tears. If you buy a bottle for the new baby and nothing for him, your four year old may feel unloved and very sad. Be careful not to treat his hurts as trivial, as they are very important to him and he needs your support. When you attend to his feelings, you strengthen his ability to face emotional pain throughout his life.

Four year olds are known to go through a period of whining and baby talk. Perhaps this is a way of showing that they are not so far from being a baby, that they have some ambivalence about growing up, or that they have a wish to be like their tiny sibling and get all the attention.

When your child talks this way, ignore it sometimes and at other times say, "Speak to me in your regular voice, so I can understand. Then I will be able to help you," and this regressed talking will eventually go away. If you overreact to it, you may enter into unnecessary, ongoing battles. When you think that your child's baby talk or whining is an emotional reaction (he is upset), try to talk with him, about what is bothering him and give him extra reassurance, hugs, and attention.

Anger

When your child was an infant, he expressed his anger physically (e.g., he waved his hands, kicked his feet, and howled when frustrated). As he grew, you may have labeled his emotion for him ("You are angry"), limited him when he hit by saying no or "Hitting is unacceptable," and encouraged him to use his words ("Say, 'I'm mad,' ") instead.

One of your child's major developmental tasks this year will be to learn to control his aggression and express his anger positively. This will be very hard for him, however, and he will still throw things or spit from time to time. You can help him by conveying that his anger is acceptable (he does not need to feel shame), limiting his negative behaviors, and encouraging him to verbalize his anger. (See Key on coping with aggression, for an in-depth discussion.)

Since your four year old is so passionate, he might love you one minute and dislike you the next. He may say, "I don't like you" or "I hate you" when you announce that it is time for bed. Try not to take these statements personally or to deny that he feels hate (it is only strong anger). These phrases are really the equivalent of saying "I'm very mad." Your child loves you more than anyone else in the world. In response, tell him, "When you say those words, I can see you are angry. You do not want to go to bed." At some point, you will need to explain that saying "I hate you" can hurt someone's feelings, especially when he says this to another child. You might want to encourage him to say "I'm angry" instead.

Your child has come a long way in his emotional development. If you keep in mind that emotional growth is an upward spiral, accept that he is still very young, and adjust your expectations accordingly, you will be more patient and capable of fostering your child's positive emotional growth.

6

SOCIAL DEVELOPMENT

Ashley sits in the circle with her arm around her best friend, Megan. As they listen to the teacher reading a story, Megan leans over and rests her head on Ashley's shoulder.

S omething miraculous happens to children's social relationships as they approach age four. Children suddenly begin to form wonderful, ongoing friendships, and they enjoy playing in groups. Your four year old would probably prefer to be with her friends than with adults or playing by herself. Do not be surprised if you hear her asking you to go on play dates all the time!

Forming Friendships

Your child loves her friends. She enjoys the same games and jokes that they do. Only a four year old can appreciate it when her companion shows her an empty cup and says, "Look! I drank my juice. Now it is down to my ankles" or shows her the green nose print she made in her clay. As a matter of fact, this year for the first time she will choose her playmates, based upon such common interests.

As your child forms these strong attachments, she will want to eat, dress, talk, and look like her friends. She may worry, too, that if her pigtails are not just right, the other children will not like her. (She's trying to establish a social identity for the first time.) When it is feasible, try to go along with her choices.

Many four year olds know how to befriend another child. One little girl will whisper to another as they stand in line at the water fountain, "You can come over to my house and play with Barbies" and will add, "OK, all right?" because she very much wants the other girl's approval. When one child is building with Legos, another may walk over and say, "I can help you. You want me to put this right there?" or will ask, "Can I play with you?" when she wants to join some game at the park.

Some four year olds, however, may have difficulty connecting with others because they are less extroverted, have had little experience with peers, are speech delayed, or have difficulty responding to social cues or norms. Such children may need you to show them how to join in.

You can suggest that your child use simple phrases such as "Can I play, too?" or "Do you want to catch the ball?" You can also demonstrate how to strike up a conversation with someone. For example, you can say, "Hello! What is your name?" when a child wanders over. In time, at her own pace, your child will internalize these approaches and find her way.

Having Fun Together

When four year olds play together, they often engage in cooperative or imaginative games. At this age, children realize that if two or more kids build together, they can make a longer railroad track or a bigger block neighborhood than they could alone (and they can share ideas while they play). If several children engage in pretend play in the backyard, there are more characters for the story: One can be the mommy, one the daddy, and one can even be their pet elephant (and it is more fun than playing alone).

As they play alongside one another, each child engages in his own fantasy (often speaking aloud). Together, the children weave a story that twists and turns. One youngster comes up with a new idea that excites the others (e.g., "Hey! This box of pebbles is really a treasure chest") and changes the direction of the story. Then everyone free-associates to the new scenario (e.g., "Let's bury it next to the tree!").

Children learn together as they play. One child may stop his bike abruptly to count the red cars passing by, and the rest of the group will stop and count, too. They often teach one another new concepts. For example, when they are swimming in the pool, one child will announce to his friends, "The Pacific Ocean is the largest ocean in the world"; another tells them while playing superheroes, "This action figure has no bones—it is made of plastic."

Getting Along

Four year olds exhibit wonderful new social abilities. When one child puts down his crayon, rather than just taking it, another will respectfully ask, "Can I use this red crayon now?" If someone wants a chance to ride on a swing, he may ask the swinger, "Can I have a turn?"

Relationships with a sibling are often stormier than with a peer because the two children share their toys, their home, and their parents, all the time. (See Key on sibling rivalry to learn how to help your children get along.)

Four year olds can be very giving. One child may say, "Look, here is a good piece of ice" while they are frolicking in the snow, and give it to her friend.

Sharing her toys will be easier for your child this year (even though she still may get possessive at times). She has a stronger sense of self than she did at three, when she may have felt that lending her stuffed lamb to someone was equivalent to giving away part of herself. Four year olds will often willingly relinquish their own ideas or follow another's in order to keep an activity going.

At four, children can negotiate problems more success-fully than the year before. They seem to have incorporated the words and approaches that their parents and other adults have used to help them settle problems. Now, with greater verbal abilities, they can use these methods with their friends.

Their performance will be uneven, however. Sometimes they will be more capable of negotiating and reasoning; at other times they may throw tantrums or resort to aggression.

Four year olds love rules. Rules help them to keep their own inner emotions and the other kids under control. In gymnastics class, when a newcomer asks, "Can I play here?" everyone says in unison, "Only four can play on this mat," and together they count the children to see whether there is room. A four year old will also instruct another, "Do not yell! You have to use words."

Sometimes conflicts arise suddenly (e.g., "I told you not to touch my dinosaur"), they heat up, and then frequently the children can resolve them on their own. They will use words to talk about the situation much more successfully than they could have at three. In the midst of the discussion, they will verbalize their feelings directly. For example, rather than cry-ing, one will say, "You're hurting my feelings." Rather than hitting, another will assertively proclaim, "I am mad" or "I am not playing with you" and walk away.

When a child is really angry about what is happening during a play date, she might say, "You are not coming to my birthday party" (even though it is the following year) or say, "Liar, liar, pants on fire" and stick out her tongue. She might also engage in name-calling: "You're stupid," "You're a butt-head," or "I don't like you." (See Key on name-calling, to learn how to respond.) If the children cannot find a solution on their own, one will usually go running off to an adult for assistance.

It is often harder for a four year old to assert himself when playing with an older child, who is usually bigger and more verbally adept. In this case, he will need the adults to give him encouragement, teach him useful skills, and intervene when he needs support. When relating to younger children, he will require guidance so that he does not become too pushy or domineering.

Sometimes, when overly stressed or excited by the play, your child may still resort to hitting, throwing, kicking, or scratching. Thus, it is important that you always remain in earshot to help your child in case of trouble.

Best Friends

This year, the concept of "best friends" is evolving. Two children can spend the whole day at school together. They sit next to each other at circle time, draw together during free choice, and swing on a tire in the yard. They enjoy whispering to each other and, in the middle of their play, kissing their friend on the cheek.

These friendships may consist of two girls, two boys, or even a girl and a boy and are the equivalent of a first puppy love. At this age, girls and boys even decide that they want to marry another child (four year olds are identifying with their parents).

As your child enjoys this new closeness, she will also have to cope with more complex interactions. Her feelings will be easily hurt as she is rejected, provoked, or insulted by her peers, and she will need your emotional support. Key 14, on helping your child build social skills, takes a look at what complex social difficulties arise for four year olds and how you can be of help.

7

~~~~~~

SEXUAL DEVELOPMENT

Parents are often shocked by their child's sexual behaviors ("He is only four!"). That is because they often assign adult meanings to these activities. But your four year old is not an adult. He is just a tiny, curious child trying to find answers and express his budding sensuality. All the behaviors discussed in this Key are part of a child's natural development.

Four year olds are often very inquisitive about the physical differences between boys and girls. Do not be surprised if your four year old takes an interest in his baby sister's anatomy (looking at, pointing and giggling, or even touching her) while they are taking a bath together. He may even reach out to grab you when you are undressed. (Many parents begin covering up more when their four-year-old child is around and cease to sleep or bathe with their child because they see that he seems to get overstimulated.)

You can say, "I see that you are curious about your sister's body. If you have any questions, come and ask me, but you cannot touch your little sister's vagina." (Since he is searching for answers, this might be a good time to read to him a children's book that explains the anatomical differences between boys and girls.)

Try to use the correct anatomical names when you talk with your child—for example, *penis* rather than *pee pee.*

Doing so conveys that you respect and value the child's sexual organs as you do any other body part. Sometimes using the phrase *private parts* is also very helpful, because four year olds understand the concept of privacy.

At this age, it is not uncommon for a parent to walk in on his child and a friend undressed, examining each other, in his room. This is a natural occurrence and is often called playing doctor. The children are just being inquisitive.

If you surprise the children in this posture, avoid any reactions that would communicate that they are bad (or they will feel guilty about their natural curiosity). Instead, simply say, "You need to put on your clothes." And when they are dressed, tell them, "It is OK to be curious about each other. We can talk about your bodies, but you cannot touch each other's private parts."

While your child is in this questioning phase and playing these games, keep the door to his room open when he has a guest, and walk in from time to time. Children who are left alone to explore one another in this way can become very anxious. They need your limits (e.g., "It is time to do something else now. How about a game of 'Candyland'?").

Four year olds can have many questions and thoughts about their own bodies. Sometimes a girl may wonder why she does not have a penis. A mother once told a story about finding her little girl standing by the toilet looking into the bowl. When asked what she was doing, she said she was looking to see if her penis fell in ("It has to be somewhere"). Another mother described her daughter's reaction to viewing her naked baby brother. She ran around the house holding a stick in front of her and saying, "Now I have a penis, too."

A little boy may wonder why he has a penis and his sister has a vagina. One little boy asked his dad, "Was my sister's penis taken away? Will someone take mine, too?"

When your child refers to these issues, be careful not to laugh at him (even though his statements may sound adorable or fantastic) or trivialize his thoughts. They are real concerns. Instead, you need to explain that girls and boys are made differently. You might even add that when they grow up to be adults like Mommy and Daddy, these differences will help them to have babies. (Of course, the next question may be, "How?" See the Key on explaining birth to your child.) Reassure your child that his or her body is beautiful.

Four year olds enjoy their bodies. They might like nothing more than to sit in a warm tub until they are all wrinkly, or strip off their clothes as soon as they walk in the door and race naked through the house wearing only their sneakers. They may also enjoy touching their genitals (masturbating). Even small babies have discovered this pleasure.

Your child may sometimes use masturbation for self-soothing (e.g., to help him fall asleep or deal with anxious feelings). At other times, he may engage in this behavior while he is just relaxing on the couch. Parents often feel uncomfortable about masturbation, because of taboos from their own childhood. They may also fear that others will disapprove of their child. It is important, however, for the parent to take an objective position. This is just a small child's behavior, like thumb sucking, that he will abandon over time.

If you see your child masturbating, you do not want to shame him for experiencing this bodily pleasure. It could cause him to feel bad about his body (and if his body is so bad, so is he) and guilty about his physical pleasure throughout life. Instead, if you are uncomfortable (e.g., when you have company), you can tell him that this is a private activity that he can do only when he's alone (he can go upstairs to his room if he likes). At other times, you can just ignore the behavior when it is not disturbing anyone, or try to distract

35

him by introducing another activity (e.g., "Let's go for a walk").

It may be hard for him to stop masturbating when you ask. Most parents notice that constantly telling a child to stop usually increases the frequency of this behavior. If you sense that this behavior is linked to some worry (e.g., Grandma is very ill), you might consider consulting a child therapist to learn how to help him with his anxiety.

It is crucial for your child's development that you communicate positively with him about his body and physical pleasure. Each person is a composite of a mind and a body, and in order for him to feel good about himself, he must be able to value both. (Fears of physical pleasure can even prevent grown-ups from being able to form healthy adult relationships.)

If you give your child a positive message in childhood, as he grows he will feel free to enjoy the pleasure of a swim in the warm, turquoise ocean; a vigorous game of tennis; and the love of a close, adult relationship. These experiences leave a person feeling like a million dollars. This is a feeling that parents want their child to experience repeatedly, unencumbered throughout life.

8

MORAL DEVELOPMENT

Maddie is lying in her bed talking to her mom. Feeling ashamed, she keeps her face covered with her blanket.

Maddie: Mom, I think I'm becoming one of those bad kids.

Mom: Why do you think you're bad?

Maddie: I can't tell you.

Mom: Did you do something that you felt was wrong?

Maddie: (Almost in a whisper) Today I was chewing on my new library book.

At four, your child wants very much to be a good child so that she will be loved by you. This is the cornerstone of her moral development. When your child pulls her cat's tail and you get mad, she may question you throughout the day, "Am I bad?" or "Do you still love me?" (She may even lie and say she didn't do it, because she fears losing your love.) Your child may beseech your forgiveness by saying repeatedly, "I try to be good."

As her parent, you may find it hard to believe that she is so concerned with right and wrong when she takes that forbidden cookie, lies about knocking down your favorite vase, or hits her brother for the millionth time. (Doesn't she know the rules by now?)

You may even get frightened when you see this behavior. You want her to know the difference between right and wrong. You want her to be honest, polite, trustworthy, giving, kind, and loving. In a scary world such as ours, where many people behave as if they have no morals, you may be fearful that she won't learn these positive values.

This fear may cause you, like other parents, to overreact and assign grown-up meanings to your child's actions. For example, when you see your four year old taking candy from a shelf at the store, you might think, "Oh my goodness—she is going to be a thief!"; sticking out her tongue at Grandma, "Oh no—she is going to be grow up to be a rude adult!"; or kicking a playmate at school, "She is going to be an ax murderer!"

The truth is, you can relax. The reason your child is still engaging in this behavior is developmental, not a lack of moral fiber. She's just not emotionally mature, as yet.

As we saw in the Key on emotional development, though four year olds have come a long way and have more control over their actions than they did at three, your child is still egocentric. She is guided by her impulses and wishes, so she might find it hard to stop jumping on the couch when she is having fun or to resist hitting her brother when he is blocking her way.

It is hard for a small child to control her impulses. Even as adults, we can identify with this difficulty when we think about how tricky it is to guide our hand past a luscious brownie when we're hungry and choose a banana instead.

It will not be until your child is five or six that she will have developed a conscience—an inner set of rules that guides her. At this point, although she will still act out and break the rules at times, she will be able to control her impulses much better and make wiser behavioral choices. This will happen as you patiently repeat your limits and she internalizes your voice (takes it inside). See the Key on limit setting and discipline, to learn some positive techniques.

Your regulations become her inner stop sign and will direct her. (Though it may be hard for you to believe, someday she will actually throw those dirty socks in the hamper!) Initially, she adopts your rules to please you and maintain your love. Later on, following these directives becomes a part of who she is.

Of course, she will continue to refine these abilities as she grows. Eventually, she will experience "anticipatory guilt" (she will not spit, because she knows she will feel bad later), will be able to observe her behavior (she will stop herself as she places her friend's toy in her pocket), and will have a heightened capacity for empathy ("I won't call my friend a name, because it will hurt her feelings").

You can help this process along by setting clear, reasonable limits and by modeling your values for her. If you want your child to be respectful, treat her, your family, and the neighbors respectfully (she is watching). If you want her to be honest, never lie to her. If you want her to be responsible for her actions and apologize, then you must apologize to her when you make a mistake. If you say please and thank you, she will be polite. Your child loves you, so she will identify with you and behave as you do. Your ideals will become hers and guide her behavior.

You must avoid double standards (e.g., that it's OK for you to hit her but she cannot hit you). Also, you cannot tell your child to value others while you are intolerant of people or a specific group of individuals. She will do what you do, not what you say.

The ultimate goal here is not the virtues themselves; it is that the child feel valuable and happy in the world.

In the meantime, sometimes she will be able to follow the rules and behave positively. She will use her words and say, "I am angry" (rather than hit) or ask for another piece of candy (rather than sneak one). If she transgresses, she may even say, "I'm sorry."

She will practice by saying the rules aloud ("It's not right to put your hand out the car window, right?") and cautioning others about the regulations ("You have to wear your bicycle helmet"). She will also report to the adults about other children's transgressions ("Brother said a bad word"). Tattletaling, though historically frowned upon, can actually be a sign that she realizes the rules are important, she is trying hard to comply, and her conscience is forming!

9

SELF-CARE

A s you watch your four year old brush his teeth, comb his hair, and wash himself in the tub, you are probably in awe at how much he can do for himself. One of the most important developmental tasks of the small child is to separate from his parents and become his own person, and your little independent fellow is well on his way!

Getting Dressed

This year, your child can put his clothes on by himself, but you will need to stand by to help in case his underwear is on backward, his shirt is inside out, he is having trouble with his buttons or zippers, or he has forgotten to put on his shoes and socks. As the year progresses and his attention span increases, he will become more detail-oriented, so his skills will improve.

Your child can slip his foot into his sneaker (you might need to loosen the laces for him) and may attempt to tie them (most four-year-old children are unable to do this success-fully). Velcro fasteners are fantastic independence boosters and must have been invented by a very clever parent!

It is important to encourage your child to participate in dressing himself so that he will sharpen these skills and build his sense of competence. If he lays back on the bed and says, "Dress me!" you might tell him, "You put on one shirt sleeve and I'll help you with the other."

Some children are adamant about choosing their clothes, whereas others take no interest. (E.g., many four-year-old girls insist upon wearing a dress each day as they are search-ing for their female identity, and some boys reject any article of clothing that is not green.)

Peer acceptance may suddenly become very important to him this year. He may refuse to wear a striped shirt because it is not "cool" (acceptable) and "the other kids might laugh."

You might allow your child to pick out his own clothes if he wants to (this encourages him to have an opinion and make his own choices). When there is a major family event, however, and you want his colors to match, or when you are in a hurry and he cannot decide what to wear, you might sug-gest that he choose between two outfits that you have pre-pared. If your child wishes to wear his bathing suit to nursery school in the wintertime, you might compromise, as some parents do, by allowing him to wear it under his outfit.

Toileting

At four, most children are toilet trained and can go to the toilet on their own. (Many will request their privacy, too!) Your child can probably reach the bathroom light and pull down his pants, and when he is finished, he may even wipe himself and flush the toilet (although many children want their parent to wipe them, even after they are five). To encourage their child's involvement, some parents tell their child, "You start wiping and then I will finish." Your child can turn the faucet on, soap up his hands, and then rinse them off and dry them.

It is well within the norm for four year olds to wet them-selves occasionally during the day and at night (even six year olds and older children will do so). Because daytime acci-dents usually take place when children are lost in their play, you might find that gentle reminders during the day can cut down on the frequency. If he wets during the night and calls for you, change his clothing and sheets in a matter-of-fact way and help him settle down again. Be careful not to scold him. He is not doing this deliberately. His arousal patterns during sleep are not yet sufficiently well developed to alert him that he needs to go to the toilet. Besides, children gain control most easily when they are relaxed and self-assured.

It is also common for four year olds who are fully trained to have setbacks and regress to a period of frequent wetting and even soiling themselves when they are ill or feeling anxious. Adjusting to a new circumstance, such as starting school or losing a babysitter, can cause such symptoms. If this occurs, have your child examined by his doctor to rule out the possibility of any contributing physical factors, such as a urinary tract infection. Try to remain calm (this will pass), and be supportive of your child (otherwise, he will feel bad about himself). Comforting your child about his anxieties and spending extra time with him can reassure him. Usually these episodes are brief and will disappear when the child is feeling more secure.

At four, some children are still not toilet trained during the day, or have never achieved dryness at night (most child development specialists agree that boys in particular can take a little longer). Usually the child's control is just developing more slowly and he simply needs more time. Sometimes, though, a child who resists training may have a strong need to assert his independence (especially if the parent is using coercion) and may even oppose his parent in other areas of their relationship, as well. In either case, he should have a complete medical exam and his doctor should monitor his progress.

Though it can be very frustrating to continue to do washloads of wet clothing and sheets at this point, it is crucial to see this as a maturational issue and not make toilet training into a battle zone. Otherwise, your child will continue to fight you (after all, it is his body and his decision). Keep in mind that children gain control most easily on their own, when they feel able, and because they want to be grown-up.

Your challenge is to remain patient and convey the utmost confidence in him. The following are some approaches that you can use with your child to help him move toward the goal.

Allowing your child to play in the house without pants and underwear will heighten his awareness of when he needs to use the toilet (with the acceptance that there will be accidents, of course). If he is willing, dressing your child in training pants or special underwear that he has picked out (rather than diapers) may motivate him to use the toilet, because he will feel more grown-up. Enrolling your child in group activities, such as a nursery school, will give him the opportunity to model his peers and he may achieve dryness.

For some children, having them go to the toilet before bedtime or taking them to the toilet before you go to sleep helps diminish bedtime wetting. You might also find that rewarding your child with a star for each morning that he is dry can lead to success.

If you find that you and your child are battling constantly or that everyone is upset, it would benefit your family tremendously to seek guidance from a mental health professional. Rest assured that no matter how long it seems to be taking, your child will not be marching down the aisle in diapers!

Eating

At four, your child can get his cereal, bowl, and cup from the cabinet (try to keep what he needs on a low shelf) and, with some supervision, prepare his own breakfast. You might use small plastic pitchers to store juice and milk so that he can pour them more easily.

Four year olds can eat their pudding with a spoon and even twirl spaghetti with their fork, but they may still need you to cut their food. It is very important to allow your child to eat on his own, even if he sometimes uses his hands or does not eat very much. Otherwise, he gets the message that he is still a baby and not really independent. He might not even be able to sense when he is hungry or full if you are always feeding him and making the decision for him. (This issue can lead to eating problems later in life.)

Just as your four year old may be particular about his clothing choices, so, too, might he have strong food preferences. He may reject any green foods, any mushy cereal, or all hot foods. Your child may have apoplexy if his mashed potatoes touch his hamburger. Food fads are also common at four. To your dismay, he might refuse to eat anything but macaroni and cheese for what seems like an eternity and then switch to eating only scrambled eggs.

Most parents will serve their child their beloved spaghetti dinner or scrape mashed potatoes from their child's hamburger. However, if the child refuses to eat his meal, demands a new hamburger, or rejects other alternatives from the dinner menu, most parents will not cook another meal. They will give their child the choice of a bowl of cereal or a peanut butter and jelly sandwich instead.

Avoid labeling your child a finicky eater. (This label can become a self-fulfilling prophecy.) He is just experimenting with his likes and dislikes as he builds a sense of himself. Respect his need to make his own choices and decisions.

In general, four year olds do not eat very much (though their appetites can fluctuate). If you are worried about whether he is eating enough, it will help to keep in mind that small children need to eat far less than adults. Nutrition should be viewed over a period of a week or two, rather than by daily intake.

If you fear that he's not getting enough nutrients at mealtimes, be sure to offer him healthy snacks, such as pieces of cheese, carrot sticks, apple slices, or homemade juice Popsicles. You might also discuss his diet with your doctor and inquire about vitamin supplements. If he is healthy and growing steadily, he is probably fine.

Your child might eat more if you involve him in planning his menu, shopping with you, and participating in meal preparation. He might enjoy cutting up vegetables with a plastic knife, kneading dough, or decorating the dinner table with colorful napkins.

Most important, do not force your child to eat or insist that he must "clean his plate." Minimize the use of food to comfort, or as a reward. At this stage in life, you are helping him to establish a positive relationship to food that will last his whole life long. You want him to eat when he's hungry, stop when he's full, experience eating as pleasurable, and learn to make positive food choices.

Be patient! Over time, his eating repertoire will increase. Just when you have given up on all the major food groups, your child will suddenly announce, "I think I'll have a salad tonight."

10

‚‚

INDEPENDENCE

In the beginning, as you held your small infant in your arms and took care of her every need, you and she were intertwined in a sublime oneness. But early on, as she exerted efforts to grasp objects on her own and flip over on to her tummy, you could see in her an innate push to become independent. With each new accomplishment, she showed gleeful exhilaration.

As we saw in the preceding key, this year your child can do much more for herself than ever before. However, you probably find yourself wondering why she takes part in her care only when she wants to or after a hard struggle.

One of the reasons your child resists is that she feels ambivalent about growing up. Along with the joy of her accomplishments, she experiences a nagging feeling of loss of the old closeness shared with you, when she was a baby. She might even ask you, "Will you still love me when I am big? Will you always hold me?"

Parents also feel this loss, with each big step (starting school) and small one (reaching the light switch) their child takes toward independence. Even though they may long for the day when their child will give up her pacifier, they can feel sad when she finally does. They miss their little baby!

It is natural for your child to play out the conflict between independence and dependence throughout her life. One minute she will be insisting that she tie her own sneakers; the next, pleading with you to put on her pants. She will confuse you with her requests as she alternates between demanding, "Feed me," "Dress me," and "Carry me" and screaming at you, "I can do it myself!" Often she will not know what she wants from you, and you will not know exactly when to step in or stand back. You will need to follow her cues as she goes through this complicated dance.

The unevenness of your four year old's behavior will show up especially when she is tired, hungry, angry, or jealous of a baby sibling. Parents also notice that when their child is turning five, or starting preschool, she is particularly fearful of being big and yearns to be a baby again. Remember, often before your child takes one developmental leap forward, she will take a few steps back.

When she asks you, "Am I still your baby?" and starts whining or talking baby talk, you can gratify her wish by taking her on your lap and saying, "You like being a baby sometimes. All children your age do." If she asks to have a baby bottle like her sister's, you might offer her one, once or twice. Usually within a few moments, she will abandon it. In the long run, she likes being bigger better than she likes being a baby!

If she says, "Dress me," tell her, "You put one sock on, while I help you with the other" (sometimes children need to be lovingly nudged along toward independence). Do not make fun of her, and try not to get angry—even adults want to be dependent and cared for at times! (See Key on raising an independent child, for other approaches.)

Another reason your child battles your requests is that a four year old needs to assert her independence. All day long, you are telling her what she needs to do or are doing things for her. She wants to have some control, too!

Most child developmental specialists explain that the child often accomplishes independence through aggression, which ranges from saying no when you ask her to sit down to running away from you when you announce, "It is time to get dressed." She is saying, "I am a separate person and I can decide what I want to do, when I want to do it."

As her parent, you may feel rejected and worry that you have done something wrong (you have not). You may be convinced that every other child in the world listens to her parents better than yours does (they do not). This struggle is a natural part of every child's development, and it is difficult for all parents and children.

You may wonder why your child responds to her babysitter's or grandmother's request to get dressed more readily than yours. It is because your child needs to separate from you, not them. She still loves you most of all, but it is through your relationship that her psychological independence is achieved.

It will be very challenging for you to manage this aspect of your child's development. If you are respectful of her individuality and find ways to avoid setting up a battle of wills with her, you will be more successful. See the Keys on daily routines, limit setting, and aggression to learn how.

11

FEARS AND ANXIETIES

One day, out of the blue, my son Michael refused to take his bath. "But you love to take a bath," said I, scratching my head. Somehow, no amount of coaxing could get my little fish into the water. Finally, through his tears Michael revealed to me that he was afraid the shark from Jaws *would show up in the bathtub! (He had seen an advertisement for the movie while he was watching a television show the night before.)*

Monsters, darkness, dogs, and circus clowns are only some of the fears that are common among four year olds (though, as we shall see, each child can have his own personalized anxieties). The child experiences these fears intensely, and they can seem as real and as terrifying to him as a nightmare appears to a grown-up.

Why are four year olds so fearful? Your tiny four year old still feels very vulnerable. There is so much about the world that he does not understand. Why is there lightning? Can children really be taken to jail if they tell a lie? Will the volcano described on the newscast suddenly destroy his neighborhood, too?

At an age when his imagination is just soaring, he still has difficulty distinguishing between fantasy and reality. In the darkness, that shadow on the floor or the creak in the hallway might just be a lurking ghost!

Not only is he frightened by the unknown in the outside world, but also he is terrified by his own internal world—his thoughts and feelings. Can his anger hurt the people he loves? (Remember, he is a magical thinker.) Can he control his aggression so that he won't get into trouble? Can he meet his parents' expectations to be more independent (e.g., not have toileting accidents during the day) when he feels so tiny and helpless and often wishes to be a baby again?

A traumatic experience such as getting lost at the supermarket, a change in his environment (e.g., a move), or a family crisis can also create fears and anxieties for the small child.

It is no wonder he gets panicky so often. As his parent, you can help your child to cope with his fears in many ways.

Whenever he expresses an anxiety, such as fear of the dark, be sure to take him seriously and acknowledge his emotion. For example: 'The dark can be scary at times." (After all, his familiar surroundings and you are absent in the darkness.)

Always convey that it is natural for your child to have fears (e.g., "Your older brother was also afraid of nightmares when he was little"). Avoid calling him a baby, trying to talk him out of any fear, or dismissing his emotion (he will feel ashamed and may keep his anxieties to himself).

Be patient, and comfort him by giving him extra hugs, speaking soothingly to him, and reassuring him that you will protect him.

The following discussion examines some of the most common fears among four year olds and includes many effective techniques you can use to calm your child.

Fear of the Dark
When he awakens frightened during the night, tell him, "I am here. You are safe." You can turn on the overhead light

and reorient him: "There's your fire engine, your books, and Quackers the duck." Demonstrate through your calmness, sense of adequacy, and optimism that his fear is manageable.

When he is more relaxed, ask your child, "What is it about the dark that frightens you?" (Always try to pinpoint why your child is afraid of something.) Once you are aware of the particular issue, such as "The dresser with the lamp on top looks like a dinosaur," you can have him problem-solve with you about how to manage the situation.

He might like to have a night-light turned on in his room or sleep with a flashlight so that he can check out the dresser whenever he needs to. If he wishes, leave the door ajar and assure him that you or his babysitter will remain nearby.

Nightmares and Monsters

Children's fears and anxieties from the day appear in their dreams at night. If parents are preoccupied with worries or problems, a child may dream about being left all alone on a street corner. The child's aggression (which he struggles to control during the day) often emerges in the form of monsters, witches, and ghosts in his nightmares. For example, his angry wish to hurt his older brother for calling him a name, or to get back at Dad for yelling at him, may take the form of an angry monster who can harm others. But the aggressive wish usually gets turned back at the child (it is more acceptable), and soon the monster is chasing him!

You can alleviate some of your child's anxiety by explaining to him that dreams and nightmares are pictures of things that he was thinking about during the day. Try to help him to talk about any worries or angry feelings he may have. During the day, provide him with constructive outlets for his emotions, and monitor his television viewing (cartoons, newscasts, and violent programs will frighten a child and can cause nightmares).

Humanizing his monsters will also diminish his fear. He can watch educational programs such as *Sesame Street* that portray monster puppets as lovable, comical characters. Before bedtime, you can even soothe your child by saying, "Don't worry—the monsters have gone out dancing tonight." (Humor often dispels terror best.)

Giving the child some form of empowerment can help him with any of his fears. You might suggest that he draw a picture of the monster from his nightmare doing something really scary. Next he can make him friendly by drawing a picture of him rollerblading with your child. Your child may also work out his fear through his play. For example, he might decide to be the king of the monsters who has invited his friends (his stuffed animals) to a tea party and then proceed to tell them how to behave (e.g., they cannot roar).

Teach your child "self-talk." He can repeat antifear statements to himself, such as, "These ghosts are not real. I can make them go away. I am safe." As he stops his scary thoughts, he will feel stronger.

At bedtime, it may be reassuring to your child if you look under the bed and open the closets to show him that there is nothing to be afraid of, or use "monster spray" (an empty aerosol can) to de-monsterize the room. He may also feel safer if you give him a cardboard sword wrapped in aluminum foil to keep by his bed (to protect himself) or hang a sign on the door: No Monsters Allowed!

Fear of Animals

Some four year olds are fearful of dogs or other animals. They are afraid because they feel a lack of control (they do not know how the animal will act). Sometimes the apprehension is related to a trauma, such as being scratched by a cat; in other cases a child will simply be modeling a parent's anxiety.

In working with this fear, you will want to desensitize the child slowly (make the dreaded object seem less and less scary). Looking at pictures of dogs in books, watching a video, or observing puppies through a store window creates a safe environment to discuss what is scary about them and to become familiar with typical animal behavior.

When you approach a dog at the park, you can ask its owner, "Is this dog friendly? Can he be petted?" Then you can model how to pet the dog, and if the child is willing, he can do it, too (even if he needs to sit in your lap). If he doesn't wish to, do not pressure him. Trusting you to respect his feelings is essential in helping him to overcome any apprehension.

Some parents decide to buy their child a small animal, such as a guinea pig, so that he can become accustomed to animals and learn how to care for a pet. Once he bonds with a specific animal by playing with it and taking care of it, he will discover that animals can be safe and fun.

Fear of Noises

At four, various auditory fears can surface for children. Loud noises, such as thunder or fire engines, may become increasingly difficult for your child to tolerate. Besides being startled, the child is disoriented (he does not understand what is happening).

Giving your child a scientific explanation can make him feel more secure. When your child is crying during a thunderstorm, explain that thunder occurs when warm air in the sky meets cold air, and that with the thunder there will be rain that will make the flowers grow. (A humorous explanation, e.g., "Someone is bowling in the sky," may also relax your child.)

You can look at pictures of fire engines in an encyclopedia and talk about why they need a siren. When your child is frightened by a continuous scary noise, such as a power drill outside in the street, you might distract him with an activity or have him put on a Walkman with his favorite music.

If you acknowledge your child's fears and give him skills to cope, he will gradually overcome his anxieties. Usually by five, children are less fearful. However, if your child's distress continues and interferes with his daily enjoyment and functioning, you might consider seeking professional advice.

12

WWWWWWWWWWWWWWWWWWWWWWWWWWWWWWWWWWWWWWWWWW

FOSTERING YOUR CHILD'S EMOTIONAL DEVELOPMENT

When Shannon burst into tears in her play group because she was eager to participate in a circle dance but was too afraid, her mom whispered in her ear, "Let's go practice the movements together in the hall."

As soon as they returned, Shannon joyfully joined in with her classmates.

It is truly wonderful to see many of today's parents behaving with so much sensitivity to their children's emotional needs. They are trying hard to address their child's feelings about starting school, prepare her for the birth of a sibling, and offer her support when the dog dies. There seems to be a growing understanding (perhaps one of the greatest breakthroughs in child rearing of modern times) that in order for children to grow up to be happy and successful in life, parents must attend to their emotional needs.

This Key will help you achieve this most crucial goal by showing you how to communicate effectively with your child about her emotions.

The Language of Emotions

Helping your child label her emotions is the first step to take in expanding her self-awareness. When she is laughing, you can comment, "You seem so happy this morning." If she sticks out her tongue, point out, "Boy, are you mad!"

When she says she loves her baby brother because he is so cute but she also hates all the attention he gets, explain to her that it is natural for children and adults to have mixed feelings (or ambivalence) even toward the people they love. These labels will help your child to identify her internal sensations and moods. Without them, she may easily become confused and frightened.

Helping her connect her emotions to an experience will also assist in her self-comprehension. For example, when she is crying after her goldfish has died, you might explain, "Children often feel sad when their pets die." Describing a series of events will also clarify the connection—for example, "I said you could not have another ice cream and you threw your doll across the room. Do you think you were feeling angry about the ice cream?"

In this way, you provide your child with a framework that helps her to organize her thoughts, and she will feel better. Even as adults, we are relieved when we can identify that the sad or anxious feelings churning inside us are caused by a specific event, such as the anniversary of the loss of a loved one.

Over time, as you talk about your child's emotions with her, she will gain the ability to identify her sentiments on her own. This growing self-comprehension will give her greater control over how she chooses to respond. Realizing that she is angry and the reason why may lead her to tell her best friend, "I am mad at you," rather than kick her.

Providing Emotional Support

It is crucial that your child know she can turn to you when she is upset, that you will be accepting of her feelings, and that you will comfort her. When she is angry because her younger brother has scribbled in her coloring book and she runs to you in tears, hold her, hug her, and listen attentively to her grievance. You might reflect back her emotion ("I can see that you're very angry"), acknowledge her feelings ("It's hard when Brother messes up your things"), and talk over how to solve the problem. She might decide to color at the table so that he cannot reach her.

In this way, you have soothed her distress, conveyed that it is OK to feel angry, and helped her find a constructive way to resolve the situation. In essence, you have provided her with a model for how she should treat her own emotions as she grows.

If a parent criticizes the child instead ("It is wrong to feel angry with your brother"), disputes the child's feelings ("You don't really hate your brother"), tries to talk the child out of her feelings ("He's only a baby"), or simply does not listen, the child may sense that her sentiments are taboo. She will decide that because the parent doesn't seem to accept her emotions, she will not let anyone know, and she will repress her emotion (push it down out of consciousness).

This form of protection is not foolproof, however, inasmuch as feelings never really disappear. They often reemerge in some unpredictable fashion. The child may experience pain deep inside, suddenly act out explosively (e.g., have a tantrum), or even develop stomachaches and other physical symptoms. If she grows up hiding her feelings, as an adult she may be out of touch with her emotions and endure chronic depression or anxiety.

The best way for children to deal with their emotions is to allow the emotions to come into consciousness, to experience them (with your support), and to find ways to express themselves positively. Your child will learn that feelings are not harmful to anyone and that she can manage even big ones.

Many parents worry that if their children cry (especially boys), they will not be tough enough to deal with life. On the contrary. Boys as well as girls will be strong only when they can work through their emotions, not avoid them.

Teaching Your Child Emotional Skills

It is important to teach your child to express her feelings in words, rather than through negative actions such as hitting, throwing things, or having a tantrum. Even as adults, when we are sad, angry, or disappointed, putting our feelings into words relieves the tension better than banging our fists on the table. Encourage your child to come and tell you, "I need a hug," "I want some attention," and even, "I am angry with you." As you listen and respond to her supportively, you will reinforce the positives of this approach.

When your child feels angry with her aunt for yelling at her, and she feels uncomfortable about telling her, you can be of help. Use role playing, puppets, or doll play to practice with her what she wants to say. For example: "This doll is Aunt Gail. Can you tell her why you are mad?" Your child might, however, prefer that you speak for her. That is perfectly fine! You can say, "Aunt Gail, Sara is angry because you yelled at her." Soon your child will be modeling you.

When she is too angry to speak about something, suggest that she stamp her feet or pound some clay. Show her how to lift a blue mood by suggesting that she ride her bicycle (physical activity can really help!), look at a book, or go on a play date. As she grows, she will use these kinds of methods to raise her spirits on her own.

Some families institute a weekly meeting at which members can discuss their feelings and resolve their differences. Meeting at a specified time once a week for this purpose establishes the importance of emotions and communication for the entire family and teaches your child important verbal skills. Consistent ground rules should be established at the outset, such as "Each person can have three minutes to talk uninterruptedly" (use a timer) and "No one is allowed to speak in a way that will hurt another family member."

Parents often wonder if all this attention to feelings really makes a difference. It does.

Small children are gaining the facility to discuss their fears about starting kindergarten, their anger about a divorce, or their sadness because a friend moved away.

The children of today will cope better because of their parents' hard work. Raising children in this emotionally attuned fashion is also vital to improving human relationships and the state of the world we live in. When people's emotional needs are attended to and they feel good inside, they do not hurt one another.

13

‹‹‹

ENCOURAGING YOUR CHILD'S INTELLECTUAL GROWTH

A s your child is developing intellectually and you interact with him as his first teacher, it is crucial to pay
attention to the quality of your educator-learner relationship (and not only to the quantity of knowledge you can
give him). For it is within the framework of your relationship
that he will establish an association to learning (enjoyable or
anxiety producing), a view of himself as a learner (competent or inadequate), and a general feeling about teachers
(helpful and supportive or critical and intimidating).

"Daddy, Look"

When your child comes to you brimming with excitement about a shell he has found, a new trick he has taught his
dog, or a question about a word he has just heard, you need
to stop, listen, and respond, even if it is to tell him, "I want to
hear what you have to say. I'll be with you in a minute."

As you smile, share in his excitement, and query him,
"Where did you find your shell?" or "How did you teach
Rusty to bring you your teddy bear?" or "What do you think
the word *independence* means?" you feed his enthusiasm for
learning about life.

When you get involved, you show him that his learning
process is important to you. In the absence of a grown-up's

response, he might feel embarrassed about his excitement, devalue his thoughts and interests, and relate to life in a more withdrawn, passive fashion.

"Why?"

In an attempt to comprehend the world, your four year old will bombard you with questions all day long and will need you to patiently explain things to him. When he asks, "Why does bread get puffy in the oven?" a simple, straightforward answer, such as "The yeast we put in it makes it rise," is all that is needed.

Sometimes the questions will be more complex or seem to come out of the blue. For example, when he is taking a bath, he might inquire, "What makes airplanes fly?"

Before jumping in to discuss the principles of aerodynamics with him, try to determine exactly what is on your child's mind. Ask him, "What are you thinking about?" or "What do you mean?" He may be wondering who drives an airplane or whether planes have an engine like a car. Once you are aware of the issue, you will be able to reply more helpfully.

Keep in mind that you do not have to know all the answers to your child's questions (it is not a test of being a good parent). If you can answer, give him a short, factual explanation. (Long-winded lectures often confuse a child, bore him, or leave him feeling inadequate because he does not comprehend, and he may even grow up afraid to ask questions.) When you are unsure, tell him, "I really do not know. Let's look it up in the encyclopedia," or take a trip with him to the library or museum. He will use these research methods on his own as he grows.

Try to be patient with your child when he grills you for the hundredth time, "Why are there rainbows?" This is the way children incorporate new knowledge.

As you discuss ideas with your child, alv[...] ful of his thoughts (never ridicule him), even v[...] "I want to be Batman when I grow up." (Don't w[...] change his mind!)

Be sure to praise your child's thinking powers. [...] validate him when he announces, "Flowers need light[...] grow" by saying, "You are very smart to understand that," he[...] will feel that he is an intelligent, capable learner and will carry this confidence throughout life.

"Let's Mix Colors!"

When your child wants to try an experiment, such as mixing colors with paints or planting seeds, listen to his ideas (even when you are afraid of a mess). Try not to automatically discourage him by saying, "Oh, that's too hard" or "Why don't you just use crayons instead?" You do not want to take away his initiative, self-motivation, or interest (important ingredients for effective learning). Besides, a project can always be modified or put off for another day.

Ask him how he would like to set up his activity and how you can be of help. Then help him devise a feasible plan and provide him with the necessary materials.

As your child works, be careful not to take over his project (even if it excites you or you want to show that you are a good parent). If you do, your child may cease to develop his own organizational and problem-solving skills. He might even begin to lose interest in learning, sit back and allow others to do for him, and ultimately lose the belief in his own capabilities. (This type of parent-child interaction can seriously interfere when a child begins to have homework).

Instead, act as his assistant. Question him, "Would you like me to put the seeds in here?" or "In which cup should I pour the red paint?" When he completes his project, always say, "Good job!" even if it is not perfect.

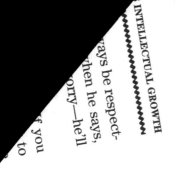

your child a new skill, such as
ent with him (and he will be
give him short, clear directions
e right answer"). Be sure to
loing fine") and to avoid criti-
therwise, he will feel inade-
;, and may even give up
pressure him into learning something
...then he shows no interest.

If your child gets stuck or makes a mistake, avoid rushing in to fix things right away (especially when he insists, "I
can do it"). Be supportive if he gets upset, and tell him,
"Don't worry, you will get it," "Everyone makes mistakes," or
"It takes time to master something new." Then inquire
whether he would like some help.

You can talk him through the difficulty, if he wishes, or
if he seems to be managing, just sit back and wait. Any learning situation has its trouble spots, and he will gain a great
deal from working through a problem on his own.

"I Love Bugs"

When your child demonstrates an interest in a particular
topic, always try to encourage him, even if his latest passion is
bugs. Go on nature walks with him, or let him choose library
books about ladybugs that you can read together. You might
even enroll him in a science class in your neighborhood.

If you show interest in and excitement about your
child's learning process and are a supportive, accepting,
encouraging teacher, your relationship will be the cornerstone of his intellectual development, leading him to success
throughout his life.

14

~~~~~~

HELPING YOUR CHILD TO BUILD SOCIAL SKILLS

"No one likes me," four-year-old Liliana announced to her parents when she arrived home from preschool one afternoon. Needless to say, her mom and dad were horrified! Memories of their own childhood wounds from rejection flooded their minds, and they worried that what Liliana was saying was really true. When they checked with Liliana's teacher at school, however, they discovered that Liliana was well liked by the other children. But she became upset because her best friend, Sophie, had been painting at the easel with another girl every morning instead of with her.

At four, your child is stepping out into a more complex social environment than ever before. More ongoing, meaningful, intense relationships are forming. As she interacts with her friends, your inexperienced socialite will encounter powerful feelings of love (she is extending her ability to love from her family to her peers), jealousy, possessiveness, and rejection for the first time.

You can be of tremendous help to your youngster by providing her with needed support, helping her understand the subtleties of what is happening in her social relationships, and suggesting specific coping strategies.

Because a child's social hurts are among the most difficult emotional issues for a parent to deal with, it will not always be easy for you. Try to maintain objectivity (you and she are separate) and to view her experience within a developmental context.

Relating to peers is just another skill that your child needs to learn about and master over time. She is only a beginner!

Sharing a Friend

As we saw in the Key on social development, this year children of similar temperament and interests will gravitate toward one another. Two children who adore dress-up might arrange for frequent play dates and spend the entire time lost in their fantasy games.

As these relationships evolve, the two friends will become increasingly important to each other. Your child may refuse to wear T-shirts that have a picture on the front because her best friend hates them, or she will adopt her companion's favorite foods.

Your child will probably develop intense loving sentiments toward her friend, and trouble can begin if her companion becomes interested in playing with someone else. Feelings of possessiveness and jealousy may erupt!

Sometimes your youngster will arrive home from preschool declaring angrily, "I'm never playing with Keisha again!" In response, you can comfort her by listening attentively, questioning her gently ("Can you tell me what happened?"), reflecting back her emotion ("You sound very angry"), and empathizing with her ("I'm sorry that your feelings were hurt").

You can further support her by acknowledging how hard it is for children to share a friend. Explain to her that because her friend wants to play with someone new, it does not mean that she does not like her anymore. Then talk with your child about what she might do next time and offer some suggestions. For example, she could tell the children how she feels or ask them, "Can I play, too?" You might help her to practice these skills through role playing or acting out the scenario with her stuffed animals. As she grows, she will learn to use these methods on her own.

If it is evident that her friend no longer wants to spend time with your child, talk with her about her sad or angry feelings. Help her to understand that small children are often friends with one child for a while and then decide that they want to play with someone new. Emphasize that there is nothing wrong with her but, for now, it is probably best for her to find another playmate.

If your child "falls in love" with someone who has never returned any interest (and she feels bad), you might try to arrange a play date for the two children, to help foster a relationship. If this is unsuccessful, explain to your child that sometimes when we like someone, he or she does not always like us. You can also give your child a personal example. You might tell her about a child you idolized who did not invite you to her birthday party. Hearing that you had a similar experience will make your child feel better.

If your child is the one being pursued by another child whom she does not want to play with, she may feel discomfort and not know what to do. You can reinforce the idea that it is OK for her not to spend time with the child, but she should try to avoid hurting her feelings. Engage your child in problem solving. She might decide to tell the other child that she is a nice person but that she likes to go on the monkey bars with her other friends.

The Third Wheel

Sometimes triangular relationships form when three children really like one another and have fun playing together. But imagine your child's dismay when she arrives at a play date eager to have fun with her two best buddies and they are each wearing a pair of jeans and tell her that she cannot play "supermarket" with them because she is wearing overalls. She might actually get in the middle and try to disrupt the play!

Another sensitive situation arises when two of the children like the third one best. In this case, there are more opportunities for one of them to be left out. A virtual tug-of-war may ensue, with both children asserting, "She is my friend" and "No, she's mine." (Be sure to set a limit on any aggressive behavior and encourage your child to talk about her feelings.)

You can inform your child that three is a hard number for relationships. Sometimes everyone can be together, whereas at other times two become better friends. Reassure her that when this happens to her, it does not mean that she is not likable or did something wrong.

Talk with your child about your own experiences as a member of a triangular friendship. For example, perhaps you once had two roommates who went off to a football game together and did not tell you about it.

Social Cliques

At four, groups of friends bonded by the same interests are often formed. Several children may enjoy playing monsters at the park together and might exclude others. (Yes, cliques can form at the age of four!)

If your child informs you that the children told her, "You can't play with us" and she is upset, she will need some perspective. You can explain that groups of friends who enjoy playing together are very common. If she wants to join their game, she might ask, but if they are not friendly, she should find other playmates.

Sometimes arranging for a play date with one of the youngsters in the group will help your child to gain acceptance. If your child is a member, it is important to support her participation ("It's nice that you have a group of friends") while instructing her ("Be sure to allow others to join in your play").

"I Want to Marry You"

At four, your child may decide that she loves a friend so much that she wants to marry him. (Isn't that what adults do?) It can be someone of the same or the opposite gender. If your child is the pursuer and is heartbroken when she receives a refusal, be there to support her; it can really hurt!

You might console her by saying, "You love Steven so much. You wish you could marry him, and you feel sad that he said no." If your child is the one pursued and is uncomfortable, talk over what she might tell the other child. For example: "I like you, but I do not want to marry you."

As you work with your child to help her negotiate these early social experiences, you will want to communicate that she will not like everyone, nor will everyone like her; that even if someone does not want to be with her, she is still valuable; and that she must always be concerned with how she treats others.

15

~~~~~~

RAISING AN INDEPENDENT CHILD

Albert is walking with his mom to nursery school. Though Mom finds it hard when it is time to say good-bye, she lets her son's hand slip out of hers. She knows her child must grow!

I t is very important to encourage your child to be independent. A child feels exhilarated when he experiences his own power and capabilities. As he grows, he will feel more secure in himself and take more risks.

When he has successfully buttoned his shirt or combed his hair, praise him (even if it's not perfect). Say, "Good job." This gives him the messages that he is capable and that being independent is good (and he will want to try more).

If he is having trouble zippering his jacket, be careful not to criticize him or jump right in and do it for him. Try to support him and give him some guidance instead. You can say, "It's hard to zip up a jacket. It takes time to learn how. Why don't you try again?" Then you can break the task down into its simplest parts—for example, "First slip the edge of your jacket into the very bottom of the zipper."

Give your child simple jobs to do around the house, such as setting the table or filling your bird's seed cup. He will feel that you view him as a competent, reliable person.

As he successfully accomplishes these tasks, he will gain confidence in himself.

When your child shows some initiative and wants to try something new, follow his lead (when it is feasible to do so, of course). For example, if he says, "I can lift the laundry basket," give him a few minutes to try, rather than saying, "Oh no—that's too heavy." If he cannot do it, tell him, "The basket is very heavy. Let's do it together. You are so strong. I need your help." If he wants to try a sleep-over at Grandma and Grandpa's, you might agree. (The fact that he is asking can be a sign that he is ready.)

Offer your child ample choices throughout the day. For example: "Which one of these shirts would you like to wear?" or "Which cereal should we buy?" Ask him his opinion about a jacket in a store window as you pass by, or what he thinks he can do when a kid at school calls him a name. Listen to him attentively when he expresses his ideas about where the family should go on a picnic or his feelings about his friend moving away. All these measures show an appreciation of his individuality and will enhance his growth.

Always be respectful of your child's separateness. Statements such as "Would you like anything more to eat?" or "I know it is hard for you when I have to wash your hair" show that you view him as a separate human being, with his own boundaries and feelings. When you acknowledge his independence, he will cooperate more.

It is important for every parent to work through his own ambivalence about his child growing up. You may feel excited that your child is growing up but sad that he is growing away from you. If you signal that it is too hard for you, however, your child will feel guilty and stay by your side.

It is difficult to let go. But it is crucial to give your child the following messages: "Go out into the world. It is safe and you can manage."

16

NURTURING YOUR
CHILD'S SELF-ESTEEM

"Mirror, mirror on the wall
What do you think of me, so small?
Am I worthy, am I good?
Tell me mirror, am I loved?"

It is in your eyes, your words, and your behavior toward her that your child forms an image of herself. In order for her to feel worthwhile and lead a happy and successful life, she will need you to convey that she is valuable and lovable. That is why handling her carefully, respectfully, and lovingly is crucial!

Parents begin to feel the weight of this awesome task soon after they hold their tiny bundle in their arms, and they are very concerned about this issue as the child grows. Most adults will say that one of their deepest wishes is for their youngster to grow up feeling good about herself. Remembering things that were said or done to them that made them feel bad when they were small, many parents strive to treat their children differently.

Helping your loved one to develop positive self-esteem is one of your most important challenges as a parent, and this Key will offer you some approaches that will help you to accomplish your goal.

Be Affectionate and Offer Praise

A touch, a smile, or a hug conveys to the child that she is adored. When you tell her, "I like the way your hair shines in the sunlight," "You look so cute in that outfit," or "I love you," she will know you care. While it seems simple, many an adult will complain that his parents never hugged him or told him "I love you," and the individual still hungers for such feedback.

Praise your little one often. Tell her, "That was a good idea" (you are smart), "I like the way you shared your raisin bread with your brother" (you are a good person), "You did a great job making your bed" (you are capable), and "I had such a good time with you" (you are likable) and she will see herself in these positive terms. She will like herself and feel comfortable and confident wherever she goes.

When your child shows you how far she can jump, comment, "That's great!" (Every new accomplishment heightens her self-esteem, especially when you acknowledge it.) When she hands you a present and says, "I made this for you!" demonstrate that it is important to you. (Anything she makes is an extension of herself.) For example, if she has made you a necklace with huge multicolored beads and thick red thread, wear it when she asks. (Just ignore the gazes of questioning onlookers!) Display her drawings on the refrigerator door, a corkboard, or some specified wall. These actions say, "What you made is important to us, and so are you."

Listen attentively, and be responsive to your youngster when she speaks. Seek her opinions, question her about her experiences, and always acknowledge her feelings and she will see that she matters. When you take time out to read to her or play her favorite game, she will feel loved. (To children, spending time equals attention equals love). If you are away from home, call her each day to show that you miss her.

Be Respectful

Always treat your child respectfully. When you say, "Can you please put your sneakers in the closet?" or "I know it's hard for you to leave your friend, but it is time to go," you convey that you value her as a separate human being, with her own needs and wishes.

Choose your words carefully. When she leaves her pajamas on the bathroom floor for the umpteenth time, avoid commonly used phrases such as "What's the matter with you?" or "How many times have I told you not to do that?" or "Are you crazy?" These words pack a mighty wallop to the child's self-esteem, for they imply that there is something wrong with her.

Labeling a youngster negatively (e.g., as dumb, stupid, a liar, lazy, a slob, slow, or clumsy), hitting her, and punishing her severely all paint a negative self-image for the child that may affect her her whole life. As a result of such childhood treatment, even a thirty-five-year-old adult will say, "Oh, I'm so clumsy! I always trip over my feet!"

It is best to relate only to the actual behavior. For example: "Pajamas need to go into the hamper." In this way, you have differentiated between the child's character and her behavior—that is, "You are good, but your behavior must change." (See the Key on discipline and limit setting, for other suggestions.)

When you and your child have quarreled, it is essential that you find a way to restore her good feeling about herself and the relationship. For example, if you have yelled at her for jumping on your bed and she has retreated to her room sobbing, you can say, "I'm sorry that I yelled. I like it better when I talk to you." (It really is OK for a parent to admit to his mistakes.) The words *I'm sorry* are magical, for they convey that your child's feelings really matter to you. You may disapprove of her behavior but you love her and do not wish to hurt her.

After your apology, you can explain your rule and discuss ways in which you both can resolve the situation better next time. Using this approach, you will also be restoring your own good feeling about yourself as a parent.

Strengthen Her Sense of Self

At four, your child may become insecure when her best friend can skate on RollerBlades or tie her shoe and she cannot. She will need you to point out that as she grows, she will be able to do these things, too. Explain to her that it takes time to learn new skills and that each person develops in her own unique way.

Emphasize that she is special—no one else in the world is quite like her! To make her feel good, you might even list her abilities for her; such as the fact that she can tell funny stories, can do great tricks on the monkey bars, and knows a lot about volcanoes.

You can also help strengthen your youngster's sense of self by encouraging her interests and talents. If she loves dinosaurs, take her to a natural history museum or borrow some books on the topic from the library. If she enjoys painting or seems to be artistic, you might consider enrolling her in an art class.

No one is a perfect parent. You will make mistakes. But if you show her ample affection and treat her with respect, she will grow up feeling good about herself. Smile often, and always remember, you are her mirror!

17

~~~~~~

NAME-CALLING

"Butt-head!" four-year-old Darryl screeched when his uncle told him not to run across the living room. His parents turned colors as the rest of the adults in the room gasped simultaneously. Their raised eyebrows seemed to imply, "What kind of perverse child are you raising?" "Where does he get such language?" "Do you speak that way at home?"

Unfortunately, Darryl's parents and the rest of the family may not know that such name-calling is a normal part of a four year old's development. Why do kids talk like this? While it is certainly true that children echo the words that they hear on television, there are also developmental reasons for children using off-color language.

Small children feel very powerless in the world. They are totally dependent upon grown-ups, and all day long adults tell them what to do. By four, they are beginning to learn that words can give them power!

One day, one of your child's friends at preschool, a cousin, or an older sibling may say "Butt-head" to him. Your child may not even know what it means, but it renders him speechless. He then turns around and uses this term on others, and lo and behold, when he says "Butt-head," everyone stops—now he has got the power. Enjoying this newfound control, he proceeds to use charged expressions over and over again.

Pee pee, doo doo, penis, vagina, stupid, idiot, and *shut up* are his favorites. Four year olds will often sit around saying these words to one another and giggling (the terms excite them and make them feel like one of the crowd).

When your child is angry or wants to be the center of attention, he may also use these expressions. For example: "You took my dinosaur. You're stupid." He may also say, "I hate you" or "I'll cut you up into a million pieces." All these phrases are the equivalent of saying "I'm mad." Remind him that saying "I'm angry" communicates his emotions more clearly, while harming no one.

Often parents will hear their child exclaiming, "Goddamn it!" in the next room. He is just mimicking someone else. Since four year olds copy everything they see and hear, it will be important for you to monitor your own speech, especially during this phase of your child's development.

When your child comes to you and tries out his latest pet expression, try not to laugh, say it is cute, or show visible shock. These reactions are an invitation for him to continue. Most experts agree that the best response to this language is a calm one or none at all.

Some parents will say to their child, "What does that mean?" (he may not know) or "Oh, I know what that means" (and explain it to their child). This neutralizes the shock waves and the fun, so the child has no need to go on. If you punish a child or forbid the use of the words, these expressions will take on a new thrill and multiply, as your child seeks revenge.

When your child calls his uncle a name in front of the family, you might talk with him privately, outside the room (away from any scrutinizing eyes). If you believe he used these words in anger, you can reinforce the idea that when he is mad, he should talk about the problem and not call people names. You can explain that he hurt his uncle's feelings with his words. He should have said, "I'm angry" instead, or come to you for help. Giving him the message that he can express his hurts directly to you or others diminishes his need for name-calling.

If your child was just having fun with his off-color words, you could have told him that he can use them only in another room, not in front of the family. You might also try to distract him from a string of *pee pee*s by saying, "Let's help Aunt Helen make the salad."

Parents find that alternating between addressing the feelings behind the words, limiting their use, ignoring them, and distracting their children helps this behavior to dissipate. Overreacting tends to make use of this language more exciting and frequent.

In the meantime, if you are searching for something to say to your shocked family members, simply tell them, "Four year olds speak this way. It's temporary."

18

SAFETY

Bernice climbs to the top of a step stool, spreads her arms, and declares, "I can fly." Lori announces, "I can go in the pool all by myself. I am a great swimmer!"

When your independent, self-confident little four year old is in motion and having a great time, it may be hard for her to stop. She is driven by her exuberance, the conviction that she is invincible, and her exciting ideas, and her immature judgment may not always protect her from harm.

A four year old can get lost, cross a busy street, or follow a dog onto an icy pond. She might even walk off with a stranger. Your child needs you to help her establish safe boundaries. Your goals will be to acquaint her with the need for caution without frightening her (it is best to leave out grim details of the horrors that could befall her) and to teach her some safety skills.

You can set up some clearly defined safety rules with her that she knows she must always follow. Explain to your child that you love her very much and do not want her to get hurt. These rules will protect her.

On the Go
When you walk down the street and your child wants to run a few steps ahead of you, if you feel it is not dangerous, your child knows she must never run into the street, and you are sure she will stop when you call her, you can give her

permission. (It is important to grant her some freedom when doing so is feasible.) Have her wait for you at a designated spot that is in sight, such as a tree, a trash can, or the corner (most four year olds will stop on a dime). If she argues and says she wants to go around the corner, that is a different story. You can explain to her, "The safety rule is that you must always be in sight. It is my job to keep you safe, so I need to be able to see you."

At the park, you can also set the same boundary: "You need to play where I can see you." Caution her, too, that there is no running in front of a swing or climbing off a see-saw before it stops.

When she is riding in a car, she must buckle up, even for one block. Whenever she is on a bicycle (as the pedaler or passenger), she must wear a helmet. (Be sure to set a good example by following these rules yourself.)

Danger Zones

If you are crossing a street or walking in a crowded area, the safety rule should be that at all times she hold your hand, the stroller (if you are pushing a baby), or even the sleeve of your shirt. (You can review this regulation as you walk to the mall.) If she fights you and runs ahead to investigate the children's carousel, tell her it is not safe. She must hold on or you will have to leave.

Instruct your child that if she gets lost, she should call out your first name (your signal). If you do not answer, she should get help from a police officer or someone who works in a store (e.g., the person behind the counter). You can practice this hypothetical event by having your child talk with a police officer and a store owner. If possible, teach your child her phone number and address, or have her carry this information.

At Home

Even though your four year old may seem to understand danger better, her curiosity and lack of mature judgment warrant your continued vigilance.

Reinforce the rule that she cannot climb up on the windowsill or any other high surface, such as a countertop, a dresser, a step stool, bookshelves, or the sink. Make sure you have window guards and a latch on your balcony door (she may believe that she can fly like Supergirl!).

Keep all medications (even chewable vitamins), sharp tools, poisonous substances, and firearms locked up. That pink bottle of cleaning fluid might suddenly look like a tasty fruit juice to her, or she might think those yellow pills on the nightstand are candy.

When your four year old is in the bathtub, she requires parental supervision at all times (children can drown in only a few inches of water). To prevent her from slipping, you might insist that the bar of soap stay in the dish and that she tell you when she wants to get in and out of the tub. She must also be told never to touch the hot water faucet.

To avoid choking accidents, keep coins, marbles, hard candies, and nuts out of your child's reach, and caution her about running in the house with food or a lollipop in her mouth.

Never leave a hot cup of coffee unattended on a kitchen counter or table. When you are cooking, use the back burners if you need to walk away, and always keep pot handles turned to the side. Disconnect and store away any electrical appliances that are not in use.

Four year olds are often fascinated by fire. Alert your child to the danger of matches, and teach her that if a fire should start, she must immediately run out of the room and then be sure to tell an adult. (A visit to your local fire station will educate your child about the rules of fire safety.)

As the year goes by, you will probably find that your four year old will be less impulsive, her judgment will improve, and she will comprehend the subtleties of caution much better. Since her safety is ultimately your responsibility, however, you will still need to continue to supervise her carefully, as she grows.

19

STRANGERS AND SEXUAL ABUSE

The issue of strangers will probably come up for your child at this age. Many four year olds are outgoing and like to tell people stories about themselves. Even if your child does not reach out to a stranger, someone might approach him.

It is crucial to educate your child about how to react to strangers so that you will protect and empower him. If you approach the topic in a calm, confident manner, as you would with any safety issue, you will help him to be cautious without making him feel unsafe or too mistrusting of others.

To begin with, ask your child if he knows what a stranger is—he might think it is someone with a funny nose! Tell him a stranger can look like Mommy, Daddy, or his big brother but is someone he does not know. Explain to him that most people in the world do not hurt others but there are some who do and must be avoided.

Inform him that, with respect to strangers, there are some safety rules he must follow so that he will be safe. He should never talk to or take candy or anything else from a stranger (unless you give him permission). He must never go away with any stranger (even if the person says he is a friend, acts nice to him, calls him by name, or says you sent him). Every day you will tell him exactly who will take care of him, and he should never leave with anyone else. If someone tries to take him, he should run quickly back to his caretaker or start screaming, "You are not my parent!" so that he can get help.

You will also need to protect your child from the potential of sexual abuse. Keep in mind that sexual abuse occurs most frequently with someone whom the child trusts or depends upon, so it is crucial that you remain alert and educate your child about what to do.

As with the issue of strangers, try to treat this matter like any other safety problem. Explain to your child that his body belongs to him. No one should touch his private parts except his parents or his doctor, when they are taking care of him. If someone does, he should tell you, immediately.

Educate him about the differences in touching: touching that feels good (e.g., Daddy hugging him), touching that feels bad (e.g., his friend pinching him), and touching that may feel funny or uncomfortable (e.g., Uncle Walter always tickling him).

Help your child to develop his own judgment about people. If he complains that his brother holds him down too long when they wrestle or that his grandmother squeezes him too hard when she hugs him, be careful not to say, "Oh, they do not mean any harm." Instead, encourage him to listen to his inner voice and to assert himself.

Emphasize that he has the right to say no and should say no when someone touches him in any way that makes him uncomfortable, no matter who it is. For example, he should tell Uncle Walter (or ask you to help him tell his uncle), "No tickling" and not worry that his uncle will get mad. If Uncle Walter is not responsive to you or your child, never leave your child alone with him. If you are present and the behavior is repeated, intervene immediately to redirect the interaction.

Reinforce the idea that your child should let you know immediately if someone bothers him and should never keep a secret about this, even if someone tells him he should. Teach your child about the difference between a good secret and a bad one. A good secret is about something pleasant (e.g., a new bike for Sister's birthday) and the whole family will know about it. A bad secret makes someone feel bad inside and is not meant to be shared with anybody. If someone tells him he should not tell anyone, he can reply, "We do not keep bad secrets in my family."

You can further ensure your child's safety by reading children's books about strangers and sexual abuse with him and practicing the safety rules. While you are walking along, you can play a game called "What if . . ." with him. For example, you can ask him, "What if you were in the park and someone offered you a Batman figure?" Have him practice saying no and pretend to run quickly back to you.

20

EXPLAINING BIRTH TO YOUR CHILD

"Where did I come from?" four-year-old Molly asked her parents one morning at breakfast. Her parents glanced nervously at each other. Was "the question" finally being asked? They took a deep breath, sat Molly down, and proceeded to relate to her the "Egg Meets Sperm" story.

Relieved that the dreaded telling was finally over, they asked Molly whether she had any questions. Looking bewildered, Molly repeated her initial query: "No, where do I come from? Samantha comes from Ohio!"

Four year olds are very curious about the way things work. They are particularly fascinated by how they were made. This topic makes parents anxious, though. For many, it can seem like a complex concept to explain.

Parents can really relax about this issue. Birth is not an emotionally laden subject for the child; nor is it sexual. For the child, it is the equivalent of inquiring, "How do you make pancakes?" Besides, the information can be broken down into simple, understandable parts and delivered over time. This Key will help you explain birth to your child.

Usually the first time your child approaches you about birth she, like Molly, will probably ask you, "Where did I come from?" As Molly's parents learned the hard way, it is best to inquire, "What are you trying to figure out?" before you launch into an explanation. Then, once you are clear about what she is trying to understand, you can say, "Where do you think you came from?" In this way, you will discover what the child's personal theory is.

Most often, children will arrive at assumptions about birth from observing their own bodily functions, especially digestion and elimination. Your child might tell you that mommies swallow a tiny watermelon seed (how else would it get in?), it grows into a baby in the mommy's stomach, and it comes out the BM place (how else would it get out?).

Listen noncritically to your childs thoughts, and when she finishes, give her a short, clear, factual answer that will correct any inaccurate perceptions. Long explanations will overwhelm her.

You can explain, "A tiny cell from Daddy's body, called a sperm, and a tiny cell from Mommy's body, called an ovum, joined together to form a baby. You grew in a special place inside Mommy's body, called a uterus." You need not give your child any more details unless she inquires further. If you follow her questions as a guide, you will ensure that you are not giving her too much information. Children understand best when they absorb one piece of the story at a time.

Children will learn about birth through a long process of asking questions (often the same one many times) and then setting off to observe the world and experiment. Your child may stare at Aunt Sally's pregnant belly and then put a pillow under her shirt to see how it feels.

Some children become absolutely enamored with one part of the description. One little girl told everyone she knew, "First I was a little dot; then I was a baby; then I was a little girl. When I was a little dot, I could not drink from a bottle."

At some point, your child will come back with new questions, such as "How does the baby get out?" Before you respond, ask her what she thinks. It may surprise you to hear such creative variations as "The mother's belly pops," "The baby comes out the belly button," or even "Pregnant women have a special zipper. When it is time, the mommy gets unzipped."

Now proceed to the real answer. Tell her, "The baby comes out of the mommy's vagina, an opening that stretches wide when the baby is ready to be born."

So far, so good. But what about the $64,000 question: "How does the father's sperm get into the mommy?" (Many four year olds and even five year olds will not be curious about this, but by the age of eight they will probably want to know.) Remember, the child is just asking casually for some information.

Parents have historically offered the "agricultural theory" to their child: "Daddy plants a seed in Mommy." Like the "stork fantasy," this account confuses children and does not help move them along toward a real understanding of the process. These fantasies can even undermine the child's trust in the parent, if the child senses they are untrue.

Instead, be simple and straightforward in response: "Daddy puts his penis into Mommy's vagina. Sperm cells come out from the penis and travel to Mommy's uterus." Children's books with pictures can greatly aid your discussion (see Suggested Readings for Children).

If you maintain a relaxed attitude and an openness to discuss any part of this wondrous tale, your child will see birth as a truly remarkable part of life!

21

"MOMMY, I WANT TO MARRY YOU!"

At four, it is common for the child in his emotional development to fall in love with the parent of the opposite sex. This has to do with his strong love for his parents and is the beginning of his forming a positive attachment to the opposite gender. For some children, this is a dramatic issue in the family; for others, it may not seem very prevalent or can be very subtle (e.g., looking lovingly into the parent's eyes or wanting to sit very close).

As a result of his feelings, your child may engage in complex behaviors. He may insist that he will marry Mommy. (Girls have a comparable fantasy about marrying Daddy.) His love is very powerful, like a teenager's first crush, so it must be handled carefully, certainly not with teasing or ridicule.

You can acknowledge your child's wish by saying, "You really would like to marry Mommy. It is OK that you wish you could. Little boys your age feel that way," and then acquaint him with the reality: "But Mommy can be married only to Daddy" (or to another adult, in a single-parent family).

Though he may get very upset about this notion, your child will also feel some relief. Deep down, he knows that he needs Mommy to be his Mommy! He may even feel some guilt about a secret wish that Daddy would go away and he would have Mommy all to himself, and fear that Daddy would be angry if he knew. The small child growing up alone in a divorced family with the parent of the opposite sex may feel especially guilty. He may believe that the wish came true because the other parent left. Your injunction may not end the fantasy, but it reinforces the reality that it will never happen.

The child may get very jealous if Mommy and Daddy kiss, and try to squeeze in between them when they are sitting on the couch or lying in bed. It is important to explain to the child that children his age often have a strong love for one parent and can find it hard to share this parent. Encourage your child to tell you if he feels this way. Reassure him that there is enough love in the family for everyone.

Your child may become very demanding—for example, "I want only Mommy to pour my cereal" or "Only Mommy can put me to sleep." During this stage, parents will often agree that Mommy can do these favored activities except when it is too hard on Mommy, or just not feasible. Then they announce to the child, "Daddy has to read your bedtime story tonight."

Daddy (or Mommy) may need a lot of support at this time because the child is openly rejecting the parent. Your child may tell Daddy, "I don't love you" or "I hate you." The parent should not take this personally (even though it is very hard). He should instead try to maintain objectivity and view this as a developmental issue.

Daddy can take heart. This four-year-old scenario gets resolved when the child relinquishes his wish to marry Mommy (sometime around five or six), identifies with Daddy, wants to spend every moment with him, and copies his every gesture (even the way he combs his hair). Girls resolve their wish by identifying with Mommy.

22

COMMUNICATING ABOUT DEATH

Your four year old is a more worldly philosopher than she was at three. This year, she will tackle some of the big questions of life, including death. At four, she is more aware of death, reacts more strongly to it, and feels a greater urgency to understand its mysteries. She wants to know: Why do people die? What happens when you die? Does everyone die? She is both fascinated and frightened by the idea of death and will look to you for the answers.

Your child may first come across death when Sweetpea, her hamster, or Old Bill, a neighbor down the street, dies, or she may learn about it when she sees the movie *Bambi*. Your child may wonder what happens to her hamster, or Old Bill, or Bambi's mother after they die. Will they "become alive again?" Since four year olds mostly think in the here and now, the idea of permanence, or "forever," is hard for them to grasp. They see death, then, as temporary. You are dead one minute and alive the next. Isn't that what happens to the coyote in the *Roadrunner* cartoons? He may get blown up by dynamite, but in the next scene he continues the chase.

Your child will play out this theme over and over again. She will point her finger; say, "Bang, you're dead"; and laugh hysterically when her dad falls on the bed. This kind of play is one way that she works out how anxious she feels about death. With her finger pointed, she is in control. She can kill others and then make them come alive at will.

If your child asks you, "When will Sweetpea get alive?" you can explain, "Remember when the plant in the kitchen with the pretty white flowers died last week? It never came back to life. When plants, trees, and flowers die, they don't come back to life again. When people or animals die, they don't come back to life, either."

As soon as your child hears that people and animals can die, she realizes that her parents and even she herself can die. She is terrified. She is so little; if you died, who would take care of her? Would it hurt her if she were to die? She may be afraid to go to sleep at night because if she does, she might die. After all, when the bad guys on television are dead, they have their eyes closed like they are sleeping. Maybe she will not wake up. She may try to stay awake because she believes that if she is constantly on the alert, you will not die. Four year olds are magical thinkers—they believe they can make things happen. If your child cannot sleep after Sweetpea or Old Bill just died, you can ask her if she is thinking about them. Then try to speak with her about her deeper fears.

You can say, "Sometimes when a person or an animal dies, children start worrying about whether or not their mommy and daddy will die and whether they will die, too." When your child asks you for the first time, "Are you going to die?" you may be very uncomfortable. This is a tough question for any parent to answer. Most parents do worry about the possibility of not being there to take care of their children, but they certainly do not want their child to be frightened about it. While it is true that you cannot guarantee what will happen in the future, for today you can give your child the answer she so desperately needs. You can say, "It will not happen for a very, very long time. You will probably be very old by then. You don't have to worry for now; it's so far away." When she asks, "Will I die?" you can say, "All people die someday, but usually when they are very, very old."

Whether or not there has been a death, your child may have nightmares about someone dying. If she does, ask her what happened in the dream and assure her that it was not real. Four year olds are still working hard to figure out what is real and what is pretend, and they need your help to tell the difference. Explain that dreams are pictures of what we were thinking about during the day, and reassure her that you are there to take care of her.

When your child asks you why Sweetpea died, give her a short explanation. Tell her that Sweetpea was very sick. You gave him medicine, but because hamsters are such small animals, he was not strong enough to get well—so he died. Still, even the simplest explanation can leave a four year old puzzled and anxious. She may worry, "If I get sick and take medicine, will I die, too?" After you give her some information, listen carefully to the child's questions to see what she has absorbed and where she still needs your help. In this case, you can reassure her that people are much stronger than small animals. They can get sick but then get better and live for a very long time.

It is also important to emphasize that Sweetpea's dying was not anyone's fault (children often blame themselves). Your child might think that because she did not fill the water bottle during the night, Sweetpea died.

If your child asks you why her older sister is crying, you can explain that people feel sad when they lose an animal or a person. It hurts for a while, but after some time it is less painful. You can also tell her that children may feel mad at a pet or a person for dying and leaving them. Encourage your child to come and tell you if she feels sad or mad about Sweetpea. If she is sad, speaking about her feelings and having a chance to honor her hamster will help. She can draw a picture of Sweetpea, dictate a story to you about him, or make a photograph album. Talk with her about her memories of Sweetpea—how she loved to hold him in her hands and kiss him and how he once crawled under the bed and they searched for him for an hour. Tell her that even though Sweetpea is dead, he will be in her heart forever, and when she thinks about her times with him, it will feel as though he were still with her.

At times, your child may seem obsessed about death. She may bombard you all year with questions at the dinner table, at the movies, or as she drifts off to sleep. This is her attempt to understand and feel secure, and it will take her some time. In her fifth year, she will begin to have a better understanding of death's permanency and the fact that people usually die when they are very old. However, it will take her many more years of development and life experience before she fully comprehends these issues. If your child has not experienced a major loss, she will probably not seem as frightened of death and will talk about it less next year. She may even approach death in a more intellectual fashion when it does come up. For example, some five year olds enjoy discussing for hours all the details of what happens after death.

Your readiness to talk with your child and your matter-of-fact approach will convey to her that death is a natural part of life: It can be talked about, and she does not have to be alone with her fears. Sharing information with her in a straightforward, supportive way will help her to face the future losses that life will inevitably bring her.

23

DAILY ROUTINES

How many times has something similar happened to you? It is 7:30 A.M. You have to leave the house in a half-hour to get your child to school on time. Your four year old is still lounging around in his pajamas in front of the television, ignoring your one-millionth plea to eat his breakfast and get dressed. Finally, out of desperation you turn off the set, he bursts into tears, and you end up screaming at the top of your lungs!

Moving your child through the daily routine is one of your hardest tasks as a parent. While you are stressed by time pressures, your needs, and your responsibilities, your four year old is constantly negotiating for five more minutes, dawdling with his sock, and generally resisting your requests ("Can't I do it later?").

Why? Your small child is not developmentally equipped to race through a hectic schedule. He is oblivious to time constraints, cannot move quickly, is busily asserting his independence, and would rather play than do anything else.

Try as you may, you might find yourself having daily arguments, often over the same five or six activities. Although there is no magic wand that will wave away these conflicts—after all, battling with you is part of his natural development—it will help if you understand the nature of the small child, readjust your expectations, and learn a few coping techniques.

Morning Madness; or, "Beat the Clock"

One of the reasons why it may be difficult for you to get your four year old out the door each morning is that small children have a slow internal time clock. They cannot be rushed. They get dressed, eat, and walk at a snail's pace. Their motor skills simply cannot be speeded up. (However, when they are running away from you when it is time for sleep, they may seem to move rather quickly!)

Your child lives in the here and now. When he awakens, he does not worry about what he has to do next, the way you do. At this age, he views life egocentrically (according to his desires). He would like to relax and have fun playing with his toys all day. (That is why at four, it really is not easy for him to respond to your need to get to work on time.)

Though these aspects of his personality may make it difficult to get him to follow a schedule, they also give him the wonderful ability to walk down the street and take a moment to smell the flowers and watch a leaf floating in a puddle of water. (Sadly, adults do not usually have the time.)

Your four year old needs you to respect his nature. It is self-defeating for you to keep yelling "Hurry up" when he cannot (it can actually make you both more irritated).

Instead, many parents work around these issues by waking their child earlier to give him extra time or by getting ready before their child is up so that they can have more patience. Some parents try to lighten their morning load by making lunches, laying out their children's clothing, and having all the book bags packed and ready by the door before they go to sleep. They might also give their child a bagel to eat on the way, arrange for him to have breakfast at school (if doing so is possible), or enlist the assistance of their spouse or a babysitter.

You might find that establishing routines for each part of the day helps your child to move along. In the morning, rather than allowing your child to watch television as soon as he rises, you can set up the following schedule: He must get up, go to the toilet, brush his teeth, dress himself, and eat breakfast, and only then can he watch television or play with his toys.

Using natural motivators such as the TV or extra playtime can get children going. You can also suggest natural consequences for noncompliance (e.g., "You will miss walking to school with your brother if you do not get ready"). Some parents give their child a reward, such as a sticker, for accomplishing one arduous task (e.g., cleaning up). After five stickers the child can pick out a small prize.

Since small children have no real sense of time, they will require you to repeat the routines to them often (e.g., "After you wash your face, it is time to brush your teeth" or "Remember, you have to get dressed before you sit down to eat"). If your child has a different routine every day—if, for example, he goes to preschool three mornings a week and to the babysitter's the other two—record his schedule on a large calendar and go over each day's activities the night before.

It is best not to stand over your child while he is dressing (doing so can be as exasperating as watching a pot of water come to a boil, and if you are too controlling, your child may begin to fight you). He also requires time to practice his skills on his own.

Stay nearby and monitor how he is doing (he may get distracted by the cat). Then assist him with a sleeve or his pants leg from time to time. In a time crunch, parents will dress their child, but it is important to encourage his independent attempts (e.g., "You put on your socks, and then I will help you with your shoes").

As you cope with your child's delays and resistance (parents can get anxious and angry), take deep breaths, count to ten before reacting, leave the room for a few minutes, or enlist extra help during the most stressful hours.

Often a child will experience changing activities or places as a separation (which brings up feelings of loss). That is why leaving the house in the morning can be so tough for kids. You are there; their toys are there; they would prefer to stay home. Here a natural motivator, such as "We better go right now so you will be on time for yard play at school," can work.

Once they are out, however, children love the world and do not wish to come home. To get your child to leave the park, acknowledge his wish by saying, "I know you wish you could stay," and then tell him, "When we get home, we can play with your new puzzle."

Evening Rush and Transitions

In the evening, when you say it is time for your child to brush his teeth, your child may ignore you and continue to play with his trains, or tell you, "I'll brush my teeth later." He may be asserting his independence! (If you bark orders like a drill sergeant, he will dig his heels in deeper.) Most people—even small children—like to march to the beat of their own drum.

That is why having a routine is so advantageous. It acts as a neutral voice, setting the course of the evening. Gentle reminders such as "Remember, as soon as you finish brushing your teeth, it will be time for your story" (which he loves) are more easily accepted than a command (though sometimes a firm "It's time" is essential).

You will find, too, that if you respect his wishes, his needs, and his activities (his individuality), he will cooperate more. Statements such as "I know you wish you could watch the end of the show" or "I will tape the rest for you" are extremely beneficial.

Listening to his reasons ("I need to finish this picture for Grandma"), explaining yours ("You need to get a good night's rest so you will be healthy"), and compromising ("You can color the hair now and finish the rest in the morning") also cut down on the necessity for him to fight you.

There are other reasons why your child may not jump to the task at hand. Transitions are difficult for small children. They have a hard time stopping what they are doing and starting a new activity (think about how uncomfortable it is for you to be interrupted when you are watching a show or reading a book).

It works best if you give your child a warning so that he can get mentally prepared for a change, such as "Five more minutes" and then "One more minute to bathtime." (Turning off the TV without advance notice will anger young and old alike.) Try to make your timing fair (e.g., "When the program is over," or "When the next commercial comes on, it will be time to set the table").

Children would rather play than do a chore. It is much more fun to color with markers than put on pajamas. Sometimes motivating your child creatively works best. For example: "I'll count to ten. Let's see if you can get your pajamas on."

Bedtime

Going to sleep at night is perceived by children as a separation. Your child is leaving you, the world, and all the activities he loves, so he will stall as much as possible. He will want "one more" of everything—a book, a drink, a hug—and will end the evening with a chorus of "I'm thirsty," "I'm hungry," "I have to go to the bathroom," or "There's a monster in my room."

Creating a bedtime ritual with children seems to ease the transition to sleep. It is important to establish a consistent bedtime for your child each night. (At four, he requires between ten and twelve hours of sleep). Before he goes to bed, make sure that your child engages in some quiet activities, such as taking a bubble bath, playing with a puzzle, or watching a nonviolent video, so that he can begin to wind down.

As bedtime approaches, give him an advance warning— "It will be time to get ready for bed in ten minutes"—so that he can finish what he is doing and get into a bedtime mood. Some parents find that it cuts down on battles, too, if they teach the child to recognize his bedtime on the clock—for example, "When the big hand reaches the top of the clock, it's time for bed." The child cannot really argue with the clock.

Once he is in bed, set aside twenty to thirty minutes to give your child your undivided attention. Reading to him, speaking with him about the day's events, rubbing his back, or singing him songs will bring him close to you and help him relax.

After your goodnight kiss, the rule may be that he does not have to fall asleep, but he must stay in bed (a night-light may comfort him). Some children will accept the separation more easily if you allow them to listen to a cassette of their favorite music while they fall asleep.

It would try the patience of a saint to cope with a four year old's constant negotiations and stalling tactics. But if you respect your child's makeup and find ways to manage his challenges rather than fight him, you and your child will get through the day more peacefully.

24

SIBLING RIVALRY

It is six o'clock in the evening. Mrs. Allen walks into her house exhausted from a long day, places her packages on the kitchen table, and begins to unload her purchases. Just then, her four-year-old daughter, Jessica, happens by, sees a huge package of Pampers protruding from one of the brown paper bags, and begins to scream: "You always buy something for baby Tyler and not for me! It's not fair!"

Parents of two or more kids hear the phrase "It's not fair!" often, whether it has to do with a complaint that you have read an extra story to one child, allowed an older sibling to stay up later than a younger one, or poured an ounce more of apple juice into one of your children's cups.

Children are constantly making a mental account of how much they are getting and how much you are giving to their siblings, in an effort to measure whether or not they are loved equally. Parents find this behavior difficult, because it implies that they are treating their kids unfairly when they are in fact trying hard to be evenhanded; it places tough demands on them, and they worry that their children are not feeling very loving toward one another.

The underlying issue that prompts siblings to behave in this competitive manner is that it is hard for children to share their parents' love. Even though a small child may think a baby brother is absolutely perfect or enjoy cuddling on the couch watching a movie with an older sibling, deep down she often longs to be loved the most (and exclusively).

Sometimes I suggest to parents that in order to understand the child's experience, they imagine what it would be like to share their spouse with another wife (or husband). How would it feel to be told, "I'm sorry, Honey, I can't come and talk to you right now; I'm watching TV with wife number two"?

Sharing parental love is a fact of life that siblings live with, and at times it raises powerful feelings of jealousy and anger for them. Sometimes they will view that extra ounce of apple juice or the package of Pampers as extra love going to a sister or brother.

When children are jealous, they may have tantrums, cry, engage in negative attention-seeking behavior (e.g., standing up on a chair at dinnertime), or even come to blows with their sisters or brothers. If your children are hitting one another, set a limit immediately. Tell them, "We do not hit anyone in our family. It is OK to feel angry, but you cannot hurt one another. You must use your words." If they continue to fight, they must be separated for a while.

If your children begin to argue in the next room, wait a few moments to see if they will resolve the problem before you go in. If they cannot, you will need to intervene to teach them some positive communication skills. When you enter, avoid taking sides (some parents always support the younger one) or the other child will feel less loved.

Have the youngsters talk about the problem. Each child can tell his side of the story (often an opposing view). You can say to each one, "Oh, I see. That's your opinion of what happened" (introducing the idea that in a family, each person will experience a situation differently but must be respected for his viewpoint).

Encourage the siblings to express their feelings and assert their wishes to each other. For example: "I'm angry. You changed the channel without asking."

Engage your children in creative problem solving. You can say, "You both want to watch your favorite show. What shall we do?" They might come up with their own viable answer, such as "Let's make a chart. Each day, we will mark off whose turn it is to choose the show." (A timer, a chart, or a rule can act as an external organizer and help siblings resolve whose turn it is to set the table or to sit in the special blue easy chair.)

As you help your children to control their aggression, assert their feelings, and negotiate solutions, they will solve problems more effectively on their own, over time.

When your little one complains that things are unfair (saying, e.g., "You never spend any time with me" after you have just read her five stories) or declares, "You like my brother better than me," you can help her by stepping into her shoes and viewing the situation from her perspective.

Sometimes parents quickly deny a child's accusations at a moment when the child is in desperate need of being heard. No matter how ludicrous the complaint may sound, there is probably some important message being communicated to you about your child's feelings and in fact there may be some truth to her grievance. Maybe you have been very involved with the baby (or an older sibling) lately and she is having trouble dealing with the shift in attention.

Have your child tell you exactly what she is mad about. Then listen carefully to her viewpoint. You can respond by saying something similar to the following: "You know, I can see what you might be feeling. We do spend lots of time feeding and diapering the baby. It feels unfair to you that we give him so much attention. You probably get mighty angry." Then explain the reality to her: "Babies need lots of care so they can grow, and when we are with him, it does not mean that we love him more than you. When you were little, we did the same for you."

After listening carefully to your child, acknowledging and accepting her perception of the events, and explaining the reality to her, it is important that the deeper issues be addressed. You should find a quiet moment to say to her, "I know that it is hard for you to share Mommy and Daddy with the baby. Before the baby was born, it was just you and Mommy and Daddy and we had all the time to give you. Now we have to share our attention. Sometimes kids feel angry or sad about this. When you feel that way, you can come and tell us and we will help you. But always remember, we have enough love for both of you."

While you can never treat your children absolutely equally, as they grow there are other measures you can take to ensure that both children feel loved, diminish the competition between them, and foster a positive relationship.

Praise each child for the things she can do, such as setting the table or drawing pretty designs, so that she will feel equally important. At the same time, try not to overemphasize one child's special talent, such as kicking a soccer ball, in front of the other sibling.

Avoid preferential treatment of siblings—for example, always having your older one clean up after dinner while the younger one plays with his toys (he probably can help, too!) or directing all your conversations to your older one at the dinner table. Do not compare your children by saying to one child, "Why can't you be neat like your brother?" or telling your relatives, "Johnny is the smart one in the family," for this greatly intensifies the competition.

Involve your youngsters in cooperative projects, such as taking care of the family's new bunny or planning a Halloween party. These joint experiences can foster a real sense of togetherness and positive feelings between siblings.

Some families hold a weekly family meeting (at a specified time) where members can discuss their feelings and clear the air and where the children can receive the assurance they need. You can establish some ground rules—for example, "Each person can speak for only three minutes" (use a timer) and "No one can hurt anyone else, physically or verbally."

Maybe Jessica's parents in our anecdote need to focus on her a little more, because their child is feeling left out. If she is willing, they might include her more in her brother's care by asking her to tie on his bib or help wash him. Her parents can also plan special outings to the zoo or a museum with her. To a child, when a parent spends time alone with her, it means the parent loves her. And maybe it is a good time for Jessica's parents to stick something special into the brown bag for her, too!

25

PARENTAL STRESS

Mom tiptoed into her son's room and tucked him in. She stood watching his angelic little face immersed in slumber. She wanted to wake him and apologize to him, because only a few moments before bedtime there had been a scene and she had yelled at him.

You mean everything to your child. Your precious jewel means the world to you. More than anything you have ever wished for, you want him to grow up happy and feeling loved. Yet with all your best intentions, you probably find yourself getting very angry and losing your cool with him at times. You may be wondering why and thinking that this is not the way it is supposed to be. This Key will discuss why the parent-child relationship can be so stressful and how parents can cope better and enjoy the experience more.

It is not easy to be a parent, especially of a small child. Children can be very difficult. Though your four year old will be a charming, adorable companion, giving you much joy and affection, at times he can also be very demanding, disobey your rules, throw tantrums, and even become aggressive.

That is because even though he enjoys being close to you, more than anyone you are the one who can gratify his needs or say no, and are always telling him what to do. It is you whom he must fight to gain his independence and some control. Most of the time, he feels safest and most comfortable with you (you will always love him) so that he can just let go!

At the same time that you must contend with the developmental difficulties your child presents to the relationship, you have your own issues to deal with.

The stresses of daily life, such as an unexpected car payment, a long list of errands, a headache, or sheer exhaustion, are hard to manage, and the tension affects your ability to be patient, to be understanding, and to find creative solutions to problems. If your child refuses to put on his jacket and it is late, you might explode! You probably find it easier to be calm with him when you are sitting on a beach, rested, and free of distractions.

Besides these external issues, each adult reacts to his own internal pressure, as well. Most mothers and fathers have an image of the type of parent they should be, fashioned by societal ideals of perfection (nurtured by the superparents portrayed on television) or their personal resolve to do things differently from how their own parents did them. If your parent was a screamer or unavailable, you are probably trying to do the opposite.

You might be striving to be eternally loving, patient, understanding, attentive, and calm. And what happens when you find yourself screaming at your child or unable to listen to his latest story about his fish? You may get upset and worry, "Oh no—I've failed as a parent!" or "Oh no—I sound just like my father!"

Feeling distraught because you have fallen short of your expectations, you might experience tremendous guilt. (Usually we then become very angry at the party that caused the guilt—our child.) Inasmuch as no one is perfect, a parent can feel guilty much of the time. These demands need to be held up to the light, evaluated for their appropriateness, and toned down.

To make matters worse, societal prescriptions for child rearing are very confusing. For example: "Give your child what he needs, but do not spoil him" or "Be consistent with him, but be flexible." Daily decisions, such as whether to buy him a toy or allow him to watch another program, make parents' heads spin.

You probably have expectations of your child, too, based upon your image of the perfect child. Perhaps you want him to be happy, brave, never angry with you, obedient, and polite (all the time). And what happens if the child is scared to death of just about everything or refuses to clean his room?

Parents can react in several ways. Many view their child as an extension of themselves (if their child is terrific, so are they). They might see the child's fear or disorganization as flaws, which means that they are flawed, too! Other perfectionist parents might immediately assume responsibility for the behavior and conclude, "It's my fault."

If an adult was very fearful as a child (or still is), or was labeled messy, and ridiculed, he might lose sight of the fact that these issues are actually developmentally appropriate for a four year old and fear that his child is turning out just like him. He may become anxious about his child's future, angry with himself for not being able to prevent these problems, and even mad at his child for his behavior. The parent might not realize that, with maturity and the parent's assistance, the child will develop better coping skills. It is crucial that parents identify these patterns and view their child as a separate, newly forming individual.

With all this pressure working you over, it's no wonder that sometimes you lose it! However, there are steps you can take to maintain control and enjoy your relationship more.

Coping with Emotions

Throughout this book, the focus has been on how to help your child cope with his emotions. The same approaches apply to you. When you are upset, try to label your emotions ("I'm angry," "I'm frustrated") and pinpoint the cause ("I'm hungry," "He's not cooperating," "He's acting just like me"). Always accept your emotions. It is OK to be angry, even at your own child. The key is to find ways to express yourself positively.

Try using some stress reduction techniques. For example, take deep breaths, relax your body, count to ten, or walk out of the room before you react. Things always get worse if you explode!

Verbalizing your feelings ("I'm nervous because we must get to the bank before it closes" or "I'm getting angry because you are not cooperating") can also reduce your tension level. Repeating your rule without emotion—for example, "We don't put greasy fingers on the window"—can help keep you on track, too! Once you start embellishing with "How could you?" you are fanning the flames of rage.

When you are having a rough day, try to grab a few moments to be alone and take a hot bath or work out (these activities relieve stress and anger). Engage your child in some quiet activity (e.g., watching a video) while you regroup your strength. Get as much help as possible. You do not need to do it all! For example, involve your spouse more or hire a teenager to help you put the children to bed.

If you do lose your temper, you and your child will feel better if you clear the air. Explain to him that you had a headache (it is not his fault) or felt frustrated by his behavior (you both need to do things differently next time), and be sure to make amends. You can say, "I'm sorry." There probably was a more positive way to handle the situation than yelling. Soon your child will model you and take responsibility for his own errors, too.

It is crucial that you resolve disputes in a way that leaves your love and respect for each other intact. You can even talk about an incident at a quiet moment, later on. For example: "Remember when you would not get dressed this morning and I screamed at you? I'm sorry I did, but I was in a big hurry. Maybe next time when I am rushing and you are not listening, I will try harder to tell you I am getting angry. What do you think you can do?" He might suggest that you count to three and then he will listen. In this way, you can both walk away feeling good about yourselves!

Be Open to Examining your Feelings

As we have seen, when an adult becomes a parent, all kinds of feelings about his childhood experiences emerge, and these greatly affect his reactions and behaviors. If you raise your awareness about your past experiences, make connections to your current behavior, and clarify what you are trying to do differently with your own child (you can make a list), you will enhance your self-comprehension and gain more control.

For example, when you are enraged with your child for not listening to you when he is watching a program and you recognize that it has to do with your anger with a parental figure who did not pay enough attention to you, you might be able to put your child's behavior into a better perspective and react more calmly.

Reevaluate Your Expectations

As a parent, you will make mistakes, for you are involved in a lifelong learning process. Above all, try not to be so hard on yourself, and enjoy your child. It is a well-accepted notion that what children need is a "good enough parent"—a parent who is available, reliable, and loving much of the time—and not a perfect one!

26

DIVORCE

Four-and-a-half-year-old Debbie sits on the living room rug, playing happily with her Barbie doll. Phil and Karen, her parents, are seated at the dining room table observing her as she carefully slips on her doll's silver evening gown and talks endearingly to her about what they'll do at the party that night. Sadness grips Phil and Karen as they think about what their decision to separate will do to Debbie. How can they help her to get through this?

If you and your spouse are getting a divorce, this difficult step has probably followed a long, arduous road gutted with desperate attempts to communicate, frequent fighting, and possibly several trial separations. Though both you and your spouse may feel pain about the loss of your family and are frightened about what will happen to your child, you are probably convinced that living apart would be less destructive in the long run for all of you.

The best chance for your child to weather the divorce in a healthy way will be you and your spouse's joint commitment to work together to ensure her emotional well-being. To prepare your child for the divorce, it is best if you both sit down with her together and explain to her exactly what is happening. This should take place several weeks before the separation, so that she can begin to adjust to the idea.

You can tell her the following: "Sometimes Mommies and Daddies cannot get along. They try very hard to talk to each other and work out their problems, but sometimes they cannot." You can even give your child an example: "Remember last week when Daddy and Mommy were yelling loudly? That was because Mommy and Daddy couldn't solve our problems."

Explain to your child that you both tried for a long time to make things better because you wanted to keep the family together, but it didn't work. Then inform her, "Mommy and Daddy are going to get a divorce," and tell her what that means. For example: "You're going to live with Mommy, and Daddy will have his own apartment, where you'll visit him. We think we'll all get along better that way. Even though we'll have two houses, you will always have Daddy and Mommy to love you."

You need to be as concrete as possible with your child about how she will be able to see her noncustodial parent, to reassure her that the parent will not be disappearing. For example, the parent can tell her, "My new apartment is a ten-minute car ride from here. I will see you every weekend, and on Mondays and Wednesdays I will pick you up from school. You will have your own room where you can sleep, with some shelves for your books and toys. I will take you to see it tomorrow."

You might give your child a calendar and mark off the days that she will see her other parent. The noncustodial parent can take her shopping to pick out a comforter for her new bed and can bring some of her toys to the new apartment.

It is crucial that both parents emphasize that the divorce is not the child's fault. You can tell your child that children often worry that had they behaved better, this would not be happening. Reassure your child that she did not cause the divorce. It is a grown-up problem between husbands and wives. You can also relate that you feel sad about the divorce and think she might feel sad and mad at times, too. Whenever she does, she can come and talk to you about it.

After these discussions, your child will probably come back to you with questions that show what she is thinking and feeling. For example, she may ask, "Who will tuck me in at night?" Because this is something that both her parents usually did together, your child reveals that she is beginning to realize that one of her parents will not be there and that she will miss the parent.

Try to address her feelings directly: "It sounds like you feel sad that both Mommy and Daddy will not be here to tuck you in at night. But when you are with Mommy, Mommy will tuck you in, and when you are with Daddy, he will. Things will be different, but we will get used to it."

Your child's behavior may begin to reflect her anxieties. For example, she may awaken at night, wet herself during the day, or act withdrawn or angry. When this occurs, it is an opportunity to discuss her worries about the divorce with her and to reassure her that everything will be OK. If these behaviors continue or are extreme, family counseling would be very beneficial. Your child might enjoy speaking with a neutral person about her feelings, and you can learn how to help your child with her adjustment. Introducing her to other young children in divorced families and reading children's books with her on the topic will also be helpful.

It is important for you to recognize that your child's acceptance of the separation is a process that will take a long time, but with emotional support, the opportunity to talk about her feelings, and the love of her parents, she can adjust to it and still have a happy life.

27

DISCIPLINE AND LIMIT SETTING

Sometimes it is helpful to think about your four year old as if he were a tiny voyager on a *Star Trek* ship who has only recently arrived here. In order to survive, he needs to learn about this new culture—what to eat, how to eat it, how to greet someone, and even how to walk down the street.

Part of his education will be in the form of limit setting. A million times a day, you will say, "You can have only one more pretzel," "You need to stop at the corner," or "Pulling the cat's whiskers is not acceptable." These rules will help him to get along successfully in life.

When you set a limit, you are not only showing him what to do and say but also helping him to cope with his impulses, fears, and anxieties. Limits make children feel safe.

While limit setting is one of your most important tasks as a parent, it is also one of your hardest. Your child will fight you often to assert his independence. You will need to be patient and repeat yourself over and over again. Ultimately, as we saw in the Key on moral development, his love for you and his wish for your approval will bring him to accept your rules. They will be his internal guide, his conscience, leading him through life.

This Key will help you communicate the rules to your child in a positive way that will invite his cooperation.

Communicate the Rule Positively

Throughout the day, you can show your child how to behave by stating firm limits in short, positive phrases, such as "*You need* to get down from the couch" or "*It's time* to get dressed." These phrases invite more cooperation than statements such as "Don't you dare jump on the couch" or "You better put your clothes on right this minute."

If he breaks a rule, be sure to let him know exactly what you would like him to do to correct himself. Children respond better to a concrete directive, such as "The books belong on the shelf" (when he is throwing them around), than to ambiguous remarks, such as "Be good" or "You better behave."

Explain Your Limit and Follow Through

Handing out orders all day long often creates resistance. When you give your child an objective reason, he will be more likely to cooperate. Rather than yelling, "Clean up your toys!" you can tell your child, "You need to put your toys away; otherwise, the pieces will get lost or broken" (this diminishes the possibility of a battle of wills). After all, if someone told you, "Stand up!" wouldn't you want to know why?

If you have stated the limit clearly and explained it and your child still is not listening—for example, he will not clean up his toys—you might break the task down ("You can put the cars away first"), offer to help ("Let's do it together"), or make the job into a game ("Let's see who can pick up the most cars").

In some situations when a child will not reason with you, direct intervention is called for. You may need to dress your resistant child when it is late, carry him out of the park when he refuses to leave, or remove from his hand the bat he is swinging menacingly at his cousin.

Relate to the Behavior, Not His Personality

Using statements such as "Kicking is unacceptable" conveys that the child's behavior is a problem. His personality is OK but his actions must change. Responding with negative phrases, such as "How many times have I told you not to leave your coat on the floor?" or "What's the matter with you?"—or calling him lazy, dumb, liar, stupid, bad, messy, or clumsy—injures the child's self-esteem, makes him angrier, and diminishes the chance that he will cooperate. Labels can even become a self-fulfilling prophecy. If someone is called a liar all the time, he will believe that it must be so, get angry at you for labeling him in this way, and even lie to get back at you!

Acknowledge Your Child's Wishes

It is natural for your child to want to own every toy in the store when you go shopping. (After all, when we are in an automobile showroom, don't we want every car that we see?) As you shop, he will say, "I want this" and "Can I have that?" Rather than calling him greedy or yelling at him for being too demanding, tell him, "You wish you could have everything you see. Look around and see what you would like us to get you next time." When you acknowledge his wish, he will feel respected as a separate individual having his own desires and will have less of a need to protest.

Many parents try to avoid such conflicts altogether, by anticipating the problem and stating the rule in advance. For example: "When we get to the store, you can choose only one small toy."

Listen and Understand

Children often have a reason for fighting you. A classic example is the little boy who insisted on being carried and who screamed when his parents tried to put him down. Had his parents not taken the time to listen to the reason—his shoes hurt—and removed the shoes, an unfortunate battle would have ensued. If your child wants to keep his door closed and he is fighting you as if his entire sense of well-being depended upon it, be sure to ask him why. He might be working on a special birthday card for you!

Reach for Feelings

When your child is spitting at you, try to figure out what he is responding to. Did you just say no about his watching a video? Then address his emotion by describing what happened. For example: "I said no to the video and you got mad. You can't spit, but you can say, 'I'm angry.' " In this way, you reinforce the distinction between an action and a feeling and channel his behavior positively. You can model this behavior for him during the day by making statements such as "I feel angry with Aunt Barbara. I'm going to call her and talk things over."

Avoid Threats and Bribes

If you constantly use threats to gain compliance (e.g., "Come to the table right now; otherwise, you won't get any dessert"), your child will learn to ignore you until you threaten him. Threats made in the heat of anger—such as "If you do not behave, you will not watch television ever again!"—are often unenforceable and the child will be trained not to listen.

Bribing him also teaches him not to pay attention until the price is right. When you say, "I'll give you a new toy if you set the table," your child may comply for the wrong reason. (He should do so because it helps the family.)

Positive Reinforcement

When your child sets the table, kiss him, hug him, or compliment his behavior ("What a good job!"). He will want to do it again! You can also diminish negative behavior when you say, "I like the way you asked me in your big-boy voice" (rather than whining).

117

Some parents use actual rewards, such as a star, when they want to encourage their child to accomplish a task (e.g., brushing his teeth). They make a chart, and each time he succeeds, he is rewarded. After receiving five stars, he can choose a special activity, such as a pizza dinner.

Time-outs

When a child is misbehaving and a conflict is escalating, a time-out can give him and his parent a chance to calm down. Time-outs can motivate children to behave better, because they do not like to interrupt their activity, feel isolated, or feel that they have lost your approval.

To begin with, inform your child of your intention: "If you spit, you'll have a time-out." Then if he spits, immediately call for a time-out (this way, the child comprehends the connection between his action and the consequence). You can say, "You are not managing here. You need to go and rest in your room so you can calm down."

Have your child sit in a quiet place, such as in a chair, on the couch, in his room, or on a bench at the park, for a few moments. Because preschoolers cannot sit for very long, the rule of thumb is one minute per year of age (e.g., four minutes for a four year old). You can use a kitchen timer.

If your child gets up ahead of time, walk him back and say, "The timer did not ring yet" (you may have to do this several times). Before your child goes back to his play, talk over the incident and help him find alternative ways to express himself. For example, you might suggest, "When you want your action figure back from your brother, you can ask for it, or come to me and I'll help you, but you cannot spit." After the time-out, the slate is wiped clean and there is no further discussion.

Time-outs are most effective when their use is limited to two to three behaviors that the parent wishes the child to change, and the parent is consistent (otherwise, children will test you or ignore you). In some cases, time-outs can lead to greater power struggles (e.g., when the child refuses to stay put). If you find that time-outs are not working with your child, stop for a while and then try again in a week or two, or use other methods, such as positive reinforcement and logical consequences, instead.

Punishment or Logical Consequences?

Many parents punish their children (e.g., take away a toy or a treat) because they believe that the child needs to "learn a lesson" for his misbehavior. Often parents take these actions when they feel frustrated, powerless, and angry and are just looking for a way to control their child. But there are problems when this approach is used with small children.

Young children are only beginning to recognize that there is a relationship between cause and effect. When you say, "No dessert" because he did not put away his toys, he may not comprehend. There is no clear connection between the two. Nor will he be more motivated to comply the next time. In fact, he may even feel mistreated, be eager to retaliate, and repeat the same misbehavior.

More severe punishments, such as spanking or washing his mouth out with soap, raise larger issues. At the moment when you want to discourage his aggressive actions, you are using aggression! Thus, you are reinforcing his behavior. We want to teach our children that there are alternative ways to solve problems.

Besides, these actions hurt your child physically and emotionally. They raise doubts in the child's mind as to whether or not you really love him and these behaviors give him the message that in life it is permissible to hurt someone you love and that he deserves to be hurt by others.

119

As a parent, it is better to count to ten, take deep breaths, say "I'm getting angry," or walk out of the room, rather than venting your anger on your child, and to try other limit-setting techniques.

Children are often motivated to follow a rule best when you discuss logical consequences with them (these are easy for a young child to comprehend and make more sense to the child than punishment). For example: "If you are not dressed in time, you will not have enough time to watch your favorite program" or "If you continue to kick the dog, I will have to put him in another room."

Limit setting is difficult for any parent. But if you establish clear, consistent rules and treat your child with respect and patience, by the time he is five you will find that your child is becoming more and more cooperative.

28

***

ANGER AND AGGRESSION

When Mom was feeding the baby, Jennifer walked over and hit her brother.

While Dad was talking on the telephone, Jake began jumping on the couch.

When she told him he could not play with his friend, Jamal threw his teddy bear at his mother.

As the parent of a four year old, you may get worried when you see your child act aggressively (especially if it is toward you). Some parents think, "Maybe she doesn't like me," "Maybe it is my fault," or "Maybe something is wrong with my child."

While in the confines of your home, you may be convinced that no other four year old acts like this. But it is not true. As we saw in the Key on emotional development, anger and aggression are a normal part of every child's development. Even though four year olds can act more grown-up and verbalize their feelings at times, most will still kick, throw things, and turn a room upside down occasionally. This usually happens when the child is upset, is asserting her independence, wants more attention, or is tired, hungry, bored, or overexcited. With these actions, your child is usually protesting that she is unhappy!

Four year olds are really not so far from babyhood, when they showed their rage by screaming and thrashing around if they waited too long for you. When your child is stressed, her control is weakened and she will regress to some form of this earlier behavior.

This year, as children face the developmental task of mastering their aggression, you will observe them playing endless games about bad guys and good guys (a symbolic representation of their internal struggle to defeat their negative impulses).

One friend will tell another, "You better stop yelling or a police officer will put you in jail." Police officers promote safety by limiting aggression, and a jail is symbolically a place to contain one's impulses. And four year olds will try hard to verbalize their needs, rather than striking out physically. For example, your child may say, "Give me back my crayon!" instead of hitting her friend.

You can help your child by setting firm limits and by teaching her the distinction between her anger, which is always acceptable (it is just a feeling), and her aggressive behavior, which must be regulated. The trick is to show her how to express herself positively.

Your greatest ally in this process will be your child's desire to maintain your love and approval: You set a limit, your child wishes to please you, and ultimately she adopts the rule. Nonetheless, this process takes place over time and requires much repetition and patience.

The following is an approach to responding effectively to your child's aggression. It is based on some of the methods outlined in the Key on discipline and limit setting, illustrated by the example of Jennifer hitting her brother.

In many situations, you will need to use only one or several of the steps. Sometimes it will be difficult to have a meaningful dialogue with your child in the midst of an incident. You may find it easier to discuss the event later on, at a quieter moment. If your child is hostile much of the time, consult the Key on the aggressive child, for additional help.

Set a Firm Limit

"Stop! That is dangerous. Hitting the baby is unacceptable. It is our job to keep the baby safe."

Small children often get overwhelmed by their aggression. If they are allowed to hurt others or break the furniture, they become frightened by their aggressive impulses. It is important to let your child know that you want her to stop. You can communicate this by using a calm, firm voice.

In the above response, when you say, "Stop! That is dangerous," you have conveyed that the child must cease her activity and you have given her the reason why. The phrase "Hitting the baby is unacceptable" affirms the important distinction that your child's behavior is the problem. She is still good and lovable. If you objectify the reason—"It is our job to keep the baby safe"—you further remove the directive from the realm of a power struggle.

If your child continues to act menacingly toward the baby, remove the baby to safety. Then you can try to distract your older child ("Why don't you take out your new Tinkertoys?"), discuss a logical consequence with her ("If you cannot stop hitting, you will have to play in another room"), or give her a time-out ("You need to stay in your room and rest until you can manage better"). For more information on positive limit-setting methods, see the Key on discipline and limit setting.

Address Your Child's Anger

"When you hit the baby, you are showing me you are angry. It is OK to be angry, but you cannot hit."

Children need their parents to help them identify their anger so that they can understand their inner world better and feel less frightened and more in control. When you say, "You are showing me you are angry," you label your child's emotion and show her the important connection between sentiments and behavior. Her action tells a story—she is furious.

If the parent accepts a child's emotion by saying "It is OK to be angry," the child will not need to hide her feelings. Otherwise, she might grow up experiencing shame and guilt about her rage and have a difficult time coping with this emotion. You are also establishing that it is safe for her to come and talk to you and depend upon you to help her manage her feelings.

Channel Her Feelings Positively

"Use your words. Say, 'I'm angry' or 'I need attention.' "

The most effective way for people to release anger is by verbalizing it. When you are incensed by your boss and you come home and slam doors or kick the dog, you may experience a release, but don't you feel best when you finally can tell someone, "I am angry" and verbalize your grievance?

If your child is too enraged to speak, you can suggest that she punch a pillow, stamp her feet, draw an angry picture, or pound some clay. Then you can try talking about her feelings when she calms down. If she will not discuss them with you directly, try using puppets. For example, you can be the bunny puppet and tell your child's tiger puppet, "I'm so angry because my brother always gets the attention. Does your brother make you mad, too?"

Connect Her Emotions to an Experience

"I was feeding the baby and you wanted my attention, too, so you got mad and hit the baby."

It is important for a child to understand the interaction of the situation that caused her response, her anger, and her aggression. Understanding this pattern will ultimately help her to stop her aggressive behavior.

In each of the anecdotes at the beginning of this Key, a precipitating event caused the child's anger and then each child misbehaved: Jennifer's mom was feeding the baby, Jake's dad was talking on the phone, and Jamal's mom refused to let him see his friend.

Parents often miss these connections (they can be hard to determine) and relate solely to the negative behavior. The initial situation soon turns into an unhappy chain of events. For example: Jennifer hits the baby. If Mom reacts angrily and punishes Jennifer by taking away her new toy, she is creating a new battle zone. (Unfortunately, Mom may not be aware that children learn most from their parents' example. If a parent takes an action in retaliation when she is angry, so will the child.)

Fired by her rage at both situations, Jennifer now calls her mom stupid. Mom gives her a time-out, and she starts running around. Parent and child have entered into a distressing loop that usually ends with both feeling helpless, frightened, and saddened by the interactions. Mom needs to stop being reactive and address her daughter's anger.

Before you respond to your child's actions, try to see what might be upsetting her. You can ask her what happened. For example: "You threw your toy at me. You are showing me you are mad. What did Mommy do to make you mad?" (Your child may find it easier to answer this concrete question, rather than responding to "Why did you do that?") You might be able to resolve the whole issue more quickly once you identify the precipitating event.

Talk About the Real Issue

"I know it's hard for you to have a new baby brother. It used to be just you, me, and Daddy, and now you have to share our love."

There is often an underlying cause to your child's behavior. If you can address it directly, your child will feel better and stop misbehaving. In a quiet moment, Jennifer's mom might use the phrases above to convey her understanding of her daughter. Jake's dad could tell him, "I can see that it is hard for you when I am on the phone and don't give you much attention. I was busy all day and you missed me." And Jamal's mom might say, "I know it is hard for you when I say you cannot see your friend. You haven't seen him all week. You really wish you could see him." If you can identify the underlying problem and talk about your child's feelings, she will have less of a need to protest.

Reassure Her and Resolve the Situation

"I have enough love for both of you."

This phrase will help Jennifer to feel less worried about sharing her parents and losing their love. Her parents might also involve Jennifer by having her sit close to Mom when she is feeding the baby, and Mom can even read her a story. Mom might also suggest that she and Jennifer plan a special day at the zoo together.

The beauty of this approach is that you have dealt directly with the issues, and your child feels understood and loved, and so she no longer has a need to misbehave. You have also given her the skills she needs to cope with her anger in the future.

29

CHALLENGING BEHAVIORS

Paula sits glued to her mother's lap at the birthday party and cries if anyone approaches. Since his arrival, Alex has kicked two children. Ignoring her mother's admonitions, Eleanor has jumped on the couch and turned on the VCR.

E very child is different and presents his own unique challenges to his parent. But some children's behaviors are harder to manage than others. You may ask why your child seems so much tougher than your friends' children. You may even feel sad or angry that your child is not easier.

Some theorists have explained these differences as related to the child's temperament. They claim that each child is born with a distinctive makeup that causes him to respond to the world in a particular way. These temperamental differences can be observed early on in a hospital nursery, where one infant will sleep all day contentedly, while another will thrash around and be hard to comfort.

In the "New York Longitudinal Study" (1956), individuals were followed from infancy to adulthood, and researchers identified nine temperamental traits: activity levels, distractibility, intensity, regularity, negative persistence, sensory threshold, approach and withdrawal, adaptability, and mood. Depending on the level of difficulty in each area (e.g., very active, very distractible, or very withdrawn) and the way in which these traits combine in the individual, the child will be easier or more difficult to manage.

It is important to become familiar with your child's temperament so that you can work more effectively with him. For example, if he is a very sensitive child and often finds his clothing uncomfortable, it might work best if he were to help you pick out his clothing. (For more information, see *The Difficult Child*, by Stanley Turecki, listed in Suggested Readings for Adults.)

Most child development specialists agree that although nature (biological makeup) has a significant role in the way a child is, so does the way in which a child is nurtured (the environment). How the parent responds to the child, as well as family events such as a divorce, the birth of a sibling, or the death of a parent, interacts with a child's disposition and normal development to shape him.

Though it is not easy, when you can, try to determine the cause of a child's behavior so that you can respond accordingly. You might ask yourself the following questions: Has he always been a temperamentally active child? Has he only recently become oppositional, since his brother was born? Is he fighting getting dressed because he is a typical four year old?

The next three keys will examine three challenging behaviors—shyness, aggressiveness, and oppositional behavior—and offer you helpful management techniques.

It is most useful to see each behavior as falling on a developmental line related to a skill that the child must achieve. For example, a child who is aggressive has not achieved impulse control as yet, but he will get there. You must be supportive and patient, accept his pace, and help guide him.

Above all, it is crucial not to overuse labels, such as naughty, wild, bad, or shy. Labeling children can lead to a self-fulfilling prophecy, because they affect the way the child sees himself and he will act accordingly. Besides, a behavior is not the whole child, and as the child matures, he will change.

Keep in mind that these are normal behaviors. The child engages in them as a way of coping with some internal or external stimulus (not to upset you!), and no matter how difficult his actions become, underneath, your child desperately wants your love and approval. If you are having a very hard time coping, do not hesitate to seek professional advice.

30

THE SHY CHILD

Some four year olds jump right in and make friends wherever they go, whereas others take a while to "warm up" or remain withdrawn. A child may stand on the side, watch longingly and still not participate, or even cry in discomfort around other children or adults.

It is important to view all these behaviors as part of the child's process of learning how to connect to others. As her parent, you must try to accept where your child is developmentally (though it can be upsetting when she is sitting on a bench alone at the park or clinging to your leg at a family gathering) and help her move forward. If you accept who she is, so will she. If she feels secure in your love, she will feel valuable and find it easier to relate to others.

Be careful not to refer to your child as shy in front of her. For example, do not tell a neighbor you meet, "She is too shy to say hello" (this will become her self-view). Instead, say, "She doesn't feel like saying hello right now," or explain to relatives whom you are visiting, "Sometimes she needs a little time to feel comfortable." Do not force your child to speak. It will embarrass her!

Be sure to provide ample opportunities for her to be with other children (preferably, children who are not overbearing). You can arrange play dates for her at her house if that is where she feels most comfortable. Enroll her in a class at the local community center or at a preschool that is run by professionals who can help her enhance her social skills.

Always prepare your child for new situations in advance by telling her who will be there and what will happen. Help her to focus on the positives of the situation, and discuss what she might like to do when she arrives. For example: "I'll bet your friend Denise will be at play group today. Do you think you might like to show her your new hair band?"

As you encourage her socialization, respect her pace. If your child wants to sit on your lap at a birthday party (even if you feel sad that she is not participating), be supportive. It really is OK. This is what she can manage for now, and this behavior will not last forever. Next year, she may be a regular socialite!

Your child may need you to model for her how to start a conversation. When someone walks over to her by the sliding pond, you can say, "Hi. This is Sara. What's your name?" Over time, your child will internalize your approaches and succeed on her own. Sometimes bringing bubbles or a ball to the park can serve as an icebreaker for a child who is having a hard time joining in.

Because the family is your child's first social group, make sure that she is a comfortable member of the group. If she always sits back, people talk for her, or she gets lost when the adults or older siblings are talking, try to bring her into conversations. She will find it easier to establish relationships.

31

THE AGGRESSIVE CHILD

At four, children are just beginning to master controlling their impulses. But some children take longer to learn this skill than others and are extremely aggressive. They will hit, kick, scratch, or bite frequently when they are angry, want attention, or do not quite know how to connect with other children. As the parent of such a child, you must find this behavior to be extremely difficult, for he is so unpredictable that his actions can be dangerous, and everyone is upset with him!

When your child is hurting another child, set a firm but unemotional limit—for example, "Kicking is not acceptable. You will hurt your friend." If you scream or tell him he is bad, his behavior will worsen. Try to distract him by suggesting, "Why don't you both play, 'Go Fish,'" and if he won't stop his behavior, lead him away from the other child to have a talk. Clarify what is bothering him and remind him, "Use your words." You might need to give him a time-out or to discuss a natural consequence with him, such as "You are having a hard time managing. If you continue to kick, we will have to leave," and follow through, if need be. In this way, you help him to contain his impulses and he will feel safer.

At times, your child probably feels very out of control, frightened, and bad about himself (people are often mad at him). He desperately needs your help in understanding what is happening. You must provide him with an emotional road map of his internal world.

Help him see the connection between his aggression and his anger (e.g., "You scratched your friend because you were mad"). Encourage him to talk to you directly about his anger or through the use of action figures. Suggest ways that he can express his anger with his friend positively. He should verbalize his feelings, call an adult, or walk away, but he cannot hurt anyone. As his ability to identify his feelings and observe his behavior grows, he will gain greater control.

Arrange play dates for him carefully (preferably, children who are nonviolent, yet assertive). If you know that your child becomes aggressive when he is overstimulated, keep play dates or visits to a party time-limited, and eliminate rough-housing and violent television shows from his repertoire.

Monitor family relationships carefully. Your child will mirror how family members express their anger. If people relate to one another in an aggressive manner, that is the way he will be. If there is someone who is hitting him, is punishing him severely, or is overcritical, he will not stop his aggression. If he hits you, step away and say, "I cannot be with you when you hurt me," or go into another room, rather than retaliating.

Try to be your child's ally despite your own anger. Be affectionate with him and convey to him that he is lovable. It is his aggressive behavior that must change, and you will help him. Have faith. By the time he is five years old, you will probably begin to see a change.

32

THE OPPOSITIONAL CHILD

S ome children give their parents a very hard time. They will run the other way when you call, constantly test you, and refuse to listen. This may have to do with the child's temperament, a reaction to a change in the family, a cry for more attention, or some patterns of interactions with the parents. Such conduct leaves parents feeling angry, powerless, inadequate, and even frightened (if the child engages in dangerous behavior). The child ends up feeling bad about herself because everyone is always yelling at her. Because you have a specific pattern of locking horns by now, change will be hard work, but it can happen.

Though your child fights your authority, she really needs you to be in control. Establish firm, consistent limits and make sure that you follow through despite her persistent protests. For example, after announcing, "You cannot eat on the sofa," you might give her a choice: "You can eat at the table, or we can put your sandwich away for later." She will feel that she has some control. If this does not work, be sure to take her hand and lead her to the kitchen table (or put the sandwich in the refrigerator). If you detect that the battle has to do with an emotional issue, such as your lack of availability because of your new job, talking with her about her feelings and spending more time with her can help her to feel less angry and become more cooperative.

At times, manipulating the environment can help you to enforce your limits, cut down on daily battles over the same issues, and ensure her safety. For example, if she is constantly breaking the rule by climbing up on the counter to get to the cookie jar, moving it to a secured cabinet, out of her reach, will eliminate this conflict.

The manner in which you communicate with a combative child can also make a difference. Try to neutralize your tone of voice when you make a request, and convey that you trust her to cooperate. Often parents who are used to a battle can unknowingly communicate that they expect one, and the child will rise to the occasion.

When approaching your child, avoid questioning her ("Would you like to wash your hands?"). Instead, state exactly what you want ("You need to wash up before dinner") and explain your requests in a concise, logical fashion ("It is healthier to eat with clean hands"). These methods invite cooperation. Use creative motivators to cut down on constant power struggles, too. For example: "After you wash your hands, we will be able to eat the salad that we made together."

If she runs away from the sink, avoid getting excited. Children with this behavior are used to connecting with you through a battle. She may be trying to rile you for this purpose. If you remain calm instead, repeat your rule objectively, and lead her back to the sink, you will begin to change your relationship.

Avoid setting up battles. Try not to say no immediately each time she asks for something; the word can signal a fight. Instead, you might repeat her request out loud ("Let's see. You want to watch television") to give yourself time to think, enlist her effort at problem solving ("We have a problem. You want to watch television and we need to go out. What should we do?"), or acknowledge her wish ("I know you really want to watch your show, but we have to get to the bank before it closes").

It is important to examine your style of limit setting. If you are too strict (always giving her commands and demanding an instantaneous response), she may be reacting negatively to assert herself. If, on the other hand, you are not setting enough limits, she may be testing you, because she wants you to react and help her to control her impulses.

Your child needs you to be "authoritative" (firm, yet open to negotiation), not authoritarian (it has to be your way, or else!). Try to show her respect ("I know you want to hear another story, but it's time to go to sleep"). Talk with her about trouble spots in the relationship (e.g., "How can we get those teeth brushed more easily?") and think about rewarding her when she does (e.g., after five nights of brushing without a battle, she can go ice-skating).

Above all, it is crucial to build up the positive side of your relationship and her self-esteem. Increase the amount of time you spend engaged in pleasurable activities with her (e.g., drawing together or putting together a puzzle), and be affectionate with her. She will realize that she can get close to you in a positive way. Praise her when she does cooperate—for example, "I like the way you are feeding the fish." She will feel better about herself and cooperate more. Even though she is very trying now, you should be optimistic. Over time, her high energy and self-directedness can make her a great success in life!

33

SUPERHERO PLAY

Who is it who dons his cape as soon as he rises and removes it only before going to sleep? It's your super four year old. Watch him as he leaps across the room and spins around, waving his invisible sword in the air. Observe him as he sneaks up on his dog, assumes a karate stance, and kicks his feet wildly in the air, until the dog runs for cover. One minute he's a superswordsman, the next he can fly through the air, while all the while he gleefully invents 101 new ways to kill the bad guys.

Parents often feel confused and worried by this play. They will ask, "Why is my child acting so violently? We are not aggressive in our home. I teach my child not to hurt other people. But look what my child is doing. He is either karate-chopping the dog, racing around the house in superhero outfits, or brandishing plastic weapons. Is it testosterone?" (Some theorists claim that boys' higher level of testosterone than girls' makes them wilder. Maybe, but no one has proven this conclusively as yet.)

Like these parents, you may be saddened to see your child so caught up in the world of superheroes. You may have tried hard to keep your child away from the clutches of commercial TV and its violence. Perhaps you have limited your child's viewing time or allowed him to watch only public television. Maybe you have forbidden him to watch cartoons or other violent shows. But even children who have never viewed these shows find themselves drawn in. They learn about superheroes at school or from friends and cousins. At four, his peer group is important to him. He wants very much to fit in; he wants to dress like the others and play with the same toys so that he will be "cool" and accepted.

But before you get angry at the neighbor's child or the kids at school, it is important to realize that children are drawn to superheroes for developmental reasons, not just commercial ones. Earlier generations worshipped characters like Robin Hood or the Lone Ranger. All of these idols have two things in common—super strength and goodness. They can handle any challenge that comes along and come out unscathed. They get into all sorts of jams and still emerge victorious over the bad guys.

Your four year old needs his heroes for several reasons. He feels more separate and independent from you than he did at three. On the one hand, he loves this new independence. He feels powerful and will proudly boast, "I can do it!" about any task at hand. He does not need you—he can take care of everything, even himself. On the other hand, the more separate and independent your child feels, the more acutely he becomes aware of how tiny he is, how scary the world is, and how much he does indeed need you to take care of him. What would happen if you went away? This need for the parent and the fact that little kids are told what to do all day long by adults ("Yes, you can have a cookie" or "No, you can't go over to your friend's house") make the child feel powerless.

But when he slips on his cape, he feels powerful again. He can do what he wants. He makes the rules. He can take care of himself. In his play, he acts tough and it can look mighty aggressive to parents. Your child may turn to this play if another child hurts his feelings, if he is pushed around by an older sibling, or to overcome his fears (e.g., if he is afraid of a robber, he can be the hero who captures the robbers; if he is afraid of fires, he can be a superfirefighter who can put out the biggest of blazes).

This superhero play helps your child to overcome his sense of powerlessness, while at the same time it is a way for him to work on learning how to take care of himself. With this awareness in mind, try to support the idea that your child does have his own abilities and can take care of himself. Praise him if he is able to dress himself, jump over a large puddle, or put a difficult puzzle together (even if he says, "Superman did it"). Ask him how he thinks he should resolve situations, rather than offering him solutions. For example, let him suggest ways to free his toy truck when it is stuck under the couch; this counters his feeling of powerlessness and diminishes his need to be someone else in order to be safe.

There is another major issue your child is working on through his play that adds a dimension to the wildness you see—the control of his aggression. Your four year old wants to be good. If he can control his aggression and other impulses that he fears are unacceptable to you, he will maintain your love and approval. In his superhero play, the fight between the good superheroes and the bad guys is really your child's internal battle, projected outward, to control his own aggression. Each time he becomes the superhero, he frees himself of his "bad impulses" (uncontrolled aggression) and is good. Each time he defeats the bad guy (who represents these impulses), he has gained the control he seeks and feels a sense of mastery.

The beauty of this play is that while your child is in the process of working out these important growth-producing issues, he has a much needed outlet for his aggression, which is channeled within a constructive framework (similar

139

to the way older kids play team sports). Though there are some female superheroes, too, many girls choose to play out similar themes through fairy tales. They identify with Snow White, who wins out over the evil queen, and Cinderella, who triumphs over her wicked stepmother.

If your child asks you to play with action figures and has you knocking them together interminably, you could use this opportunity to help your child along developmentally. Though you generally want to follow his lead, sometimes you can ask him, "What's happening? Why are they fighting? Who's winning? What does it mean to be a good guy? What other solutions are there to fighting?" You can playact with his figures or use puppets to show how the two sides can talk about the problems, rather than fight. Reinforce the idea that good guys can get angry (it does not make them bad) but they need to learn acceptable ways to express themselves. Communicate to him that people use their natural aggression positively, to assert their opinions, to compete in the world, and to separate and become independent.

If your child's obsessive superhero play becomes overwhelming, you can set some limits. For example, if your child insists that you call him Batman, make a rule that you will do so only in the confines of your home (certainly not in the supermarket or at a family gathering). Set a limit on the number of supertoys that you will buy in a week or a lifetime, and define clearly where he can wear his superhero clothes—for example, he cannot wear them to school or when the family goes to a restaurant. In this way, he will not be tempted to play the superhero in inappropriate places. If your child has a strong reaction to these limits, you can compromise with him. For example, although he cannot wear his whole superhero outfit to school, maybe he can wear the shirt underneath his school clothes or carry his cape in his knapsack and leave it in his cubby.

Though it is hard to view so much aggressive play, try to think of superhero play as similar to a team sport. As your child builds a trap for the bad guys with his friends or strategizes about an upcoming battle, he is channeling his aggression constructively, learning how to assert himself, cooperate, compete, fight fairly, and win and lose. Because kids can get overexcited when they play superheroes, end up bullying one another and getting hurt, strict ground rules should be established about avoiding contact and not hurting anyone. To further ensure safety, set limits on where children can play (e.g., on a mat) and for how long. When the pretend play becomes real fighting, end it by suggesting they play "Candyland" or eat a snack instead. It might make you feel better if you read to your child about real heroes with whom he can identify, such as Martin Luther King, Jr., who helped the world without hurting others.

Try to view your child's sometimes zany superhero play with respect and humor. This play gives your child an important opportunity to master the struggle between good and bad impulses, between independence and dependence, and to work on other vital issues. If you set appropriate limits, explain your view of violence, and suggest alternative routes for resolution of conflicts, your child's play will not harm him. Be patient. Though each child's development follows its own unique path, five year olds tend to be more in charge of their aggression and are more confident about their independence. Your child will slowly drift away from superhero play and may soon be trading in his cape and sword for a bat and ball or a game of checkers.

34

PLAY DATES

Tiffany is very excited. Arlene is coming to her house for a play date after preschool. Tiffany has been waiting for this event for three whole days. Ten minutes into their play, however, Tiffany breaks out in tears and goes running to her mom. "Arlene has to go home," Tiffany says. "She won't play dress-up with me!"

A play date is more complicated than meets the eye. As soon as your child knows a friend is coming to her house, she might begin to plan out exactly what they will do. If her latest passion is putting on a pair of her mommy's heels and acting out *Cinderella*, she may expect her friend to be interested, too.

When her companion arrives and would rather put together a puzzle or draw on her chalkboard, watch out! Finding this hard to accept, your child might insist upon her choice of activity, and an argument could ensue.

Parents often get upset when they see their child acting bossy with a friend (telling her what to do or how to do it). In this case, they might view Tiffany's insistence upon playing dress-up as inappropriate behavior for a hostess. But she is just a small child, after all, and we have seen that for days she has had her heart set on sharing her favorite game. Besides, it is natural for any small child to want to run the show when the play date is at her house. She is feeling quite important and very territorial!

In the situation above, you might wait a few moments to see if the children will arrive at a compromise. (It is best that you or another adult always stay nearby during a play date to help the four year olds resolve such issues.) If they cannot find a solution, you can tell your child, "I know that you want to play dress-up with your friend because you love it so much, but you have to think about her wishes, too. Why don't you both take turns at choosing an activity?"

You might even set a timer to help them determine when it is time to switch. This reinforces the notion that cooperation is the best way to keep the fun going. If her companion is still not in agreement, you can suggest that your child put off playing dress-up until after she leaves. Explain to her, "Sometimes we choose a game that will please our guest."

If you find, however, that your child never seems to assert her wishes and is bossed around by this particular friend or other children, you can coach her. Suggest that she tell her friend, "Last time we played your favorite game. Today let's play mine."

(If your child has a younger sibling who always wants to join in on his big sister's play date, your older child might feel resentful. You can explain to your younger child that his sister needs her privacy, or negotiate with your older child to include him for a short time, if she is willing. Parents find that it helps both children when the parents invite a friend for the younger child at the same time.)

A dispute may arise if your child's visitor decides that she wants to use your child's new set of stickers and she refuses. Do not worry if your child still gets possessive of her things at times. Though it may appear that her behavior is equivalent to being selfish, it really is not the same thing.

Remember, at four she is a newcomer to real sharing. Besides, it is not easy for a small child to have someone browse through her room and touch all her belongings. (Even an adult might feel uncomfortable under similar circumstances.)

Try to avoid this problem by planning ahead. Have your child put away her favorite toys before her friend comes over and leave out only those that she is willing to share. Even after this weeding-out process, however, her feelings may suddenly change and you might hear her exclaim, "Mom, she's touching my tea set!"

When such a scenario occurs, suggest to your child that she tell her friend that she is not ready to share her tea set today. If your child tries to prevent the other child from playing with any of her toys, you can explain to her that she really must let her friend use some of her things. Otherwise, her friend will be unhappy and may not want to visit again. (Wouldn't your child be sad if she couldn't play with her friend's toys?)

Sometimes a child's guest may want to engage in activities that she does at her house (e.g., jumping on the bed or watching scary movies) but these behaviors are not acceptable in your home. You or your child can tell her friend, "In our family, the rules are different. We cannot jump on the bed or watch scary movies."

Though four year olds can negotiate problems much better than they could at three, a tug-of-war might still erupt over a toy. In anger, one child may call the other "pee-pee head," the other child might start hitting, and one or both of them could end up crying. The children will need you to mediate the quarrel.

As you enter the room, set a limit. Say, "Stop. There's no hitting or name-calling allowed in our house." Avoid taking sides (you really do not know exactly what has happened). Comfort the child who is upset (or both of them), and listen to each child's feelings and point of view. If the stories differ, just acknowledge that each child seems to have a different opinion.

After you elicit as much information as possible (this whole process may take only a few minutes), you can engage the children in joint problem solving: "You both want to play with the same Barbie doll. What shall we do?" Maybe the two playmates will come up with their own creative solution (e.g., "Let's take turns dressing her"). Otherwise, you can make a similar suggestion.

If the particular activity in which the children are engaged starts getting out of hand, establish clear limits. For example, when the children are fighting over who is winning at the game "Chutes and Ladders" (small children often feel a strong need to be the winner), you can go over the rules with them or join in as the scorekeeper. When the children are becoming wild as they are enacting their favorite super-heroes, you might announce, "It is time for Supergirl and her pal to choose a quiet game."

When the children badly need refocusing, parents often bring out some Play-Doh, offer the children a drink of juice, or take them for a walk. The children might also benefit from separating and playing on their own for a while. If nothing seems to work, it is probably time for them to finish playing. (If the two children fight frequently, you should keep their play dates short or encourage your child to invite other friends.)

Children often have a hard time saying good-bye when a play date comes to an end. The two friends have been having such a good time that they may even stall by hiding under the bed!

You can ease their separation by giving them some advance notice—for example, "Arlene's mom will be here in fifteen minutes" (ten, five, and two minute warnings are often needed, too). This way, the children can finish what they were doing and prepare themselves to say good-bye.

Your child might part from her buddy more readily if you tell her that she can call her friend on the phone the minute she gets home, or when you say, "Don't worry. You can get together again next Monday," and mark it on the calendar.

35

~~~~~~

WRITING, READING, AND MATH SKILLS

"Look, Mommy! That sign says, Stop!" your little four year old announces, as all onlookers gaze at him in astonishment. "How old is he?" they want to know. At such a moment, you feel proud of your child (he is a genius, of course!) and you feel good about yourself as a parent (you have produced this prodigy and have gotten him this far).

One of the most thrilling parts of being a parent is watching your child's learning skills evolve, especially when he starts to read, write, and do math. In essence, he has been experimenting with and exploring these skills since day one, through his play, through his daily interactions with you, by watching educational programs such as *Sesame Street*, and by observing others. He will continue to progress at his own pace in these areas, driven by his self-motivation, as he searches for increasingly sophisticated ways to communicate with others, copies you, and tries to figure out the puzzles of life.

As his parent, you may wonder what your role should be in helping him to learn these most basic skills (after all, you want to give him the best foundation possible for his future success). Some educators believe that small children should have formal training in these areas (using workbooks, flash cards, and other methods of rote learning). Most experts, however, are convinced that experiential learning, such as learning the names of fruits by handling them while playing store, fueled by the child's self-motivation, works best.

Your main goal as your child's partner in learning should be to nurture his natural interest in reading, writing, and mathematics (not push him or hold him back) and to help him build a positive association to these skills.

How? Always follow his lead, and be there to convey that these activities are pleasurable. Provide him with information, assistance, and encouragement, and find natural, enjoyable ways to stimulate him. If your child is enrolled in preschool, you should expect the same approach.

Writing

Your child may become interested in writing the letters of the alphabet this year. This desire may be spurred on by educational television programs, observation of his older sibling or cousins, or his wish to sign his name at the bottom of his drawing.

In actuality, he has been preparing for this moment for a long time. As he drew designs and shapes on paper (or even in the sand) and said, "Look at my cat," he was learning that a written symbol could stand for something real. This year, as he scribbles you a short note and begins to write letters and words, he is making the important connection that what he has to say can be recorded, too.

At first, he will write large, capital letters without much thought as to where they are placed on the page. (His name may even take up a whole page!) As the year progresses, however, your child may learn the lowercase letters and be able to fit all the letters of a word on one line.

He will practice these letters over and over again and may get frustrated if he cannot succeed (especially if his older sibling can). You will need to give him gentle encouragement by saying, "You'll get it," "Keep trying," or "It's hard to write letters."

His letters may be awkward or even backward at times, and he will forget how to write the letters he knows. Your job is to show him how to write a desired letter, tell him what letter comes next in a word, and, most of all, not criticize him. Just allow him to have fun! Otherwise, he will feel inadequate, develop a negative association to writing, or stop completely. (This can lead to ongoing problems when he starts his formal education.)

Do not worry if your child does not show any interest in writing this year, or it's too hard for him (even if five of his friends can write their names). He may spend his time making intricate drawings or Lego constructions instead, which builds the motor skills he will need for writing. Next year, he may suddenly pick up a pencil and begin to write!

The best way to stimulate your child's interest in writing is to reinforce the idea that writing is fun and that it has a purpose—to communicate thoughts and feelings to others. Here are some simple activities that you can use to stimulate his interest:

1. Have him draw a picture and dictate a story to you about it. As he speaks, he can watch you as you jot it down. Then read it back to him.

2. Pretend that he is the waiter in a restaurant, and he can write letters or scribble as you order.

3. Suggest that he send a thank-you card to his grandparents for his new toy, and help him to spell a few simple words. If he has learned the sounds of the letters already and seems interested, he might even use inventive spelling (writing a word the way it sounds, such as *lv* for *love*). Today this is a well-accepted method of teaching children how to write, because it immediately gives them the ability to communicate.

Reading

Children's earliest experience with reading is being read to. This is an extremely pleasurable experience for your child. He has your full attention, feels close to you, and enjoys the sound of your voice and looking at the pictures. When you talk about the characters together, laugh at the funny things they say, and share in the suspense of waiting to see what happens at the end of the story, your child is building a positive association to books.

As you read to him, he becomes familiar with the sounds of the words. If you read the same book over and over again, at his request, he will soon memorize the story (especially if the words rhyme). He will be able to sit with the book and tell the story to you, or to his stuffed animals, by looking at the pictures (avoid correcting his rendition!).

At four, he may already know the alphabet (thank goodness for *Sesame Street* and the alphabet song!) and he will begin to identify letters everywhere—in his name, on a sign in a store window, or in a word on the cereal box. He may even recognize some words, too, like *cat*, in *The Cat in the Hat* or *dog*, in *Go Dog Go*.

This new ability might come about after seeing a word repeatedly, recognizing its shape or its place on a page, or being cued by a picture, the content of the story, or the first letter of the word. Your child may also have developed a budding capacity to sound out words.

Your role is to continue to convey a love of books to your child. Keep reading to him (you can make it an enjoyable bedtime routine), and discuss the new information and ideas in the story ("Why do you think the boy is crying?" or "Where do you think the duck is hiding?"). He will see that reading is fun and a way to gain knowledge about new animals, people, and places.

If you keep plenty of books in your home, your child sees you reading, and you make frequent trips to the library with him, you are modeling for him the importance of reading.

You can further encourage his involvement in the following ways:

1. Your child can make his own book by drawing pictures, dictating a story to you, and stapling all the pages together.
2. As you walk along, read the signs on the street out loud. If he asks you what one says, you can help him to sound it out phonetically (e.g., "o-pen").
3. Play word games with him, such as "Give me a word that rhymes with *hat*" or "Besides *Mommy*, what other words start with the letter *M*?"

Mathematics

Believe it or not, at this very moment your child is learning some important math skills. If he is building with blocks, he will see that two small unit blocks equal a large one and that if you put a heavy block on top of a light one, it will tumble. When he is playing school with his stuffed animals, he may count out the number of books he needs for all his students until he gets it right.

In your daily interactions with your child, he is also learning some important math concepts. For example, when he is helping you to carry the groceries into the house, you will say to him, "Take the lightest bag" and he will compare the weights. When he is helping you set the table, you may tell him to take four forks and four spoons out of the drawer and he will get them.

Historically, mathematics has had a fear element attached to it for many people. You can establish a more positive association for your child by making math into a game and referring to it as solving a puzzle:

151

1. In everyday conversation, you can encourage your child to problem-solve by asking him, "How many cups of juice do you need for all your friends?" or "If your sister weren't coming to dinner, how many forks would you need to put on the table?"

2. As you walk through your neighborhood, point out the different shapes you see. When you get home, cut out some geometric forms for your child and ask him if he would like to make a collage or a picture of the neighborhood.

3. When your child is in the bathtub or by the sink, you can do some water experiments. Give him a plastic cup and he can compare the sizes of different containers by the amount of water each can hold.

Try to be patient with your child, and respect his own developmental pace. For a long time, he may remain uninterested; forget letters, numbers, and words; and make mistakes. Do not pressure him. It is more important that he love learning than that he learn early!

36

~~~~~~

THE VALUE OF PRESCHOOL

If you peek into your child's preschool classroom, you will see happy children playing. In the dress-up corner, Shana, Sharon, and Joseph are wearing hats and scarves and are pretending to prepare dinner. Michael and Meredith are busily painting colorful designs at the easels, while nearby, Jonathan and Richard are sitting on the rug building a huge Lego space station together. Nina, the teacher, weaves her way in and out among the youngsters, smiling here, answering a child's question there, and carefully observing how each child is doing.

The beauty of nursery school is that it provides small children with the opportunity to interact with peers in a structured group environment (one that has specific rules, routines, and values), under the guidance of a warm, supportive professional.

The teacher helps the children to build their social and emotional skills, stimulates their love of learning and their self-expression, and teaches them how to function effectively as a group member. Many early childhood educators believe that these are the important goals of a quality preschool program, because they are the cornerstones for building a happy and successful life. Programs that focus primarily on academic skills at this age are developmentally premature. (This Key refers to schools that are built upon the former ideals.)

Another plus of preschool is that the teachers are trained to detect any area in which a child requires extra assistance (e.g., eyesight, following rules, or impulse control), and through a joint effort of the parent and the teacher, the problem can be remedied early on.

Most parents find that once their child enters nursery school, every aspect of her development is enriched!

Social Skills

The teacher's positive phrases and respectful behavior set the tone and standards for the social interactions within the classroom. Building upon what they have learned at home, the children absorb the teacher's approaches and the school's values over time. Then, as they practice their new skills with one another, the preschoolers become teachers, too. They model positive behavior for their friends and constantly instruct one another about the rules.

Your child will learn all about taking turns and sharing at school. She will need to stand in line to use the sink and wait patiently until it is her turn to pour herself some juice.

As she sits in the circle at group time, she will be instructed, "We all need to sit quietly and pay attention to one another," and her listening skills will improve. She will enhance her ability to express herself as she is encouraged to answer questions, state her opinion, or stand up and tell the class about her special toy. When she sets the table at snacktime or reads quietly on the rug while the music teacher sets up, she will expand her capacity to cooperate.

Throughout the day, the teacher will reinforce positive behavior by saying, "Good listening," or "You're taking turns so nicely." As we can clearly see, the teacher's role is crucial in fostering the children's social development. (That is why when you are choosing a school, the quality of the teachers is of utmost importance.)

Emotional Skills

At preschool, your child will develop emotionally. She will gain greater impulse control when she is told, "Crayons are for coloring, not for throwing," or "When you are angry, use your words." The teacher will often provide her with emotional support ("It must have been sad for you when your fish died") and show her ways to express her feelings ("Would you like me to help you write a story about him?"). Or one of her friends might put her arm around your child to comfort her. Here, too, a loving, respectful teacher who is concerned about feelings will set the tone for the classroom.

Your child will develop her capacity for empathy when the teacher explains to her, "It made María feel sad when you told her that you hate her." In an atmosphere so focused on and accepting of feelings, your child will grow in her ability to tell others how she feels, too (e.g., "You hurt my feelings when you said I couldn't play").

The children often talk about feelings as a group, too. When the teacher reads the story *Beauty and the Beast*, she will ask them, "Why do you think the beast was so sad?" Using puppet play, she may demonstrate how to cope with the daily emotional issues they face. For example, when Ms. Duck and Ms. Rabbit puppets won't let Mr. Bear play, he might choose to tell them how sad he feels or go and find another playmate.

It is the teacher's job to help the children negotiate conflicts. She might hold each child's hand gently and have them talk to one another about their feelings. For example, she will say, "Tell Landon why you are angry" or ask them, "What do you think you can do to solve the problem?" until they have arrived at a peaceful solution. The children will walk away with a skill that they can use next time.

155

Cognitive Development

Most preschool educators believe that small children learn best by doing—that is, using their senses, not through formal education. They believe that requiring young children to sit and trace letters in workbooks or memorize flash cards can leave small children feeling bored, constricted, pressured, and even negative about learning.

Preschoolers need to move around the room and explore materials according to their own interests and creativity. As the children pretend to be a storekeeper, build Tinkertoy robots, or mold dinosaurs out of clay, they are experimenting with important concepts—shapes, sizes, weights, numbers, and so on—that will help them develop their abstract thinking. When they talk about their ideas and share information with their friends or ask the teacher questions, they further enhance their understanding.

Through group learning, all these concepts are reinforced in natural ways. For example, at circle time the teacher might say, "Who can tell us how many children are missing today?" or "Everyone who is wearing a blue shirt can now move a little closer to see the turtle."

The children participate in hands-on group projects, such as mixing colors or planting seeds. When they learn in this concrete way, the new information is easily integrated and the youngsters will even want to repeat the same experiments at home.

Children's early writing and reading skills are often stimulated according to interest or need. As a child makes a card for her grandfather, she might ask the teacher, "How do you spell *love*?" When a child asks what her job is for the day, the teacher might respond, "Can you find your name on the job chart?" The teacher accepts what the children can do and never pressures them.

By the time children leave nursery school, most have attained the essential skills they will need to begin their formal education.

Following Rules and Routines

While a preschool includes lots of time for free play, there still is a basic structure to the day—for example, free choice, group meeting, yard play, snack, rest, and then dismissal time. This structure makes children feel safe and comfortable (they know exactly what to expect). It also lends itself to following rules and cooperation. For example: "We have to clean up now, so we can all go out to the yard."

Sometimes parents wonder why their child can follow routines more easily at school than at home—it's the same schedule every day and everyone is doing it!

Independence

At school, your child will become more independent. She will observe how another child zips her jacket or buttons her shirt and copy her just to be more grown-up.

The teachers encourage the children to toilet themselves and throw away their cup and napkin after a snack. They also give them special jobs and responsibilities, such as feeding the fish and leading the line.

Once again, parents will scratch their heads, wondering why their child can wipe herself at school, yet insists that the parent do it for her at home, or why the child willingly cleans up her toys in the classroom but tells her parents, "You clean my room."

The answer is that at school there is peer pressure to be big. At home, there are other forces at play. Parents often do a task for their child for expediency's sake (who has the time to wait while a child struggles endlessly with her zipper?). Besides, your child has a vested interest in remaining your baby and is conflicted about whether or not she wants to be independent. Rest assured, though: Some of her new independent skills will be brought home, too!

Attending preschool in itself fosters independence. The child feels strong because she is functioning on her own, away from home.

Self-esteem

When your child hears, "Good job," "We missed you when you were sick," or "I like your ideas" on a daily basis, she will feel that she is competent and a valued member of the group.

The end result of her preschool experience should be that she feels good about herself, socializes well, trusts authority figures, and, very important, enjoys going to school!

37

~~~~~~

CHOOSING A PROGRAM

As a parent, you are looking for a nursery school where your child will be safe, will be well taken care of, and will grow and develop a positive feeling about himself and the world. This Key will provide you with guidelines that will help you in your search for a quality program and assist you in preparing your child for his new adventure.

Interview with the Director

During your meeting with the director (or another school representative), ask about the program's philosophy. In our earlier discussion of the value of preschool, it was evident that choosing one that focuses primarily upon the social and emotional development of children is highly recommended, because these skills are the foundation for a happy, successful life. Discuss the school's expectations of the children, too, to see whether they are age appropriate: Homework for a four year old is not; nor is perfect behavior.

Clarify other issues, as well, such as the staff's qualifications. Make sure that the teachers have had professional training in early childhood education. Ask about parent-teacher communication. You should be able to visit and talk with the teacher about your concerns. Find out about the school's approach to discipline. The staff should use only positive, respectful approaches and never yell at or hit a child. Ask how the school handles a child with a behavioral problem. The staff should be supportive and willing to work with parents to develop joint strategies to help the child. Inquire about school safety and health measures. There should be standard procedures for responding to an accident, an illness, or a fire. You should also address how this institution will help your particular child to grow. For example, what steps will the teachers take to help your withdrawn child become more outgoing?

The Teachers

As we have seen in the previous key, The teacher will have a tremendous impact upon your child's development and sense of well-being.

Ask to observe the teacher your child would have were he enrolled. Watch to see whether the teacher smiles often and seems to genuinely love children. As she (or he) moves around the room, does she touch a child gently on the shoulder or stoop down to a youngster's eye level from time to time, to converse with him? Does she listen attentively, patiently, and respectfully and offer the children praise, support, information, and encouragement when these are needed?

Is the teacher aware of what is happening in the room? Does she move in quickly to set limits with an aggressive child—for example, "Pushing is not permitted"? Will she involve a child who seems withdrawn by suggesting, "Would you like to roll some clay at the table?" or help two children to resolve a conflict positively by saying, "You both want the swing. You need to take turns"?

Does the teacher discipline without attacking a child's self-esteem and provide the child with a helpful skill to use next time by saying, "You can say, 'I need more room,' but you cannot push"? Is she conveying an excitement for learning to the children? Her manner of speaking and her creative ideas should stimulate the children's interest and involvement.

While no teacher is perfect, select a school with a staff with whom you would feel comfortable if you yourself were starting nursery school. (*Note*: At this age, the ratio of teachers to children should be at least one teacher and one assistant for sixteen to twenty children).

The Curriculum

The curriculum should be geared to young children's interests (e.g., nature, the family, holidays, and the neighborhood) and needs. Small children should have plenty of opportunities to move around, freely choose activities, and use materials creatively. The program should be well structured (e.g., outdoor play, snacks, free-choice time, a group meeting, and then dismissal), because young children feel most secure when they know exactly what to expect.

Because preschoolers learn best through doing, there should be a wide assortment of activities for hands-on experience that will help young children to grow. As you look around the room, you should see a dress-up area for pretend play (with an assortment of old clothing and props), where children can use their imagination, express their emotions, and learn about the different roles people play. There should be easels and plenty of art supplies (e.g., paper, markers, crayons, clay, scissors, and paste) so that the children can be creative as they experiment with various materials and ideas, along with a wide array of blocks, puzzles, and manipulative toys (such as Duplos, Legos, and Bristle Blocks) to stimulate the children's thinking, problem-solving abilities, and fine motor skills. A library, a rest area, a science corner, and a water-play table are also important ingredients of a quality preschool program.

It is essential that the daily schedule include class meetings and group projects so that the children can experience group learning, and daily physical activity done in a secure outside area. Music and dance activities should be part of the program, too, because they greatly enhance children's self-expression.

161

Physical Space

The facilities must be safe. Check to see whether there is a smoke detector in each room, there are easily accessible fire exits, cleaning fluids are stored out of reach, and emergency phone numbers are posted near the telephones. There should also be special safety surfaces under and around outdoor equipment.

The rooms should be bright, clean, well organized, and spacious (crowded children can become unhappy and aggressive). Toys and other play materials should be stored in labeled bins on shelves at the children's eye level so that they are easily accessible. Each classroom should be divided into clearly defined areas, such as block building, dress-up, and group meeting time, and portray an environment of learning (e.g, colorful charts on the walls, labels on interest areas, and a fish tank).

When choosing a school, make sure that the children seem happy and involved and that your particular child will fit in (if he's very quiet or aggressive, look for a smaller, calmer environment with more individualized attention). Most of all, use your own feelings as a guide. Choose a school that you would be happy to attend!

Preparing for Preschool

Since this is your child's first preschool experience, he will need to know what to expect. While searching for a program, you probably will make a preliminary visit to the nursery school with your child. The administration might suggest that your child play in the classroom for a while so that he can meet the teacher and feel more comfortable in the environment. (This experience will ease his transition later on, when the class actually begins). If there is no formal policy about your child's participation, you might make such a request.

Some schools will arrange for a home visit during the summer so that the child can bond with the teacher and she can better understand the child's and parents' needs. Another program might send the child a postcard to foster an attachment.

At home, you can prepare your child by reading him some children's books that describe preschool. (See Suggested Readings for Children.) It is important to outline for your child exactly what the first day will be like. You might talk with him about the separation from you and suggest that if he gets sad, he can tell the teacher. In fact, reinforce the idea that whatever he needs, he should tell the teacher, who is there to help him. (You can even use role playing to practice how.)

If you can, arrange for some play dates with other children who will be attending your child's class, to help your child forge an early connection. As the starting date approaches, try not to talk too much about the event or play up the fact that he is so big now. He may become anxious and worry that he is really too little to manage.

If you present school as a safe, fun place to be, one where your child will learn many new things, over time he will adjust, and certainly blossom from the experience.

38

STARTING SCHOOL

It is the first day of nursery school. Four-year-old Audrey arrives with her mother. She spots an easel in the corner, races over to it, and starts painting a face. A few minutes later, Gregg enters the room. He clings to his mother's side as he watches some children rolling clay at a table with the teacher. Next, Brianna is carried into the classroom in her father's arms, crying inconsolably. She refuses to let her dad put her down.

Starting school is a developmental milestone for children—a step toward growth and independence. With each move forward that a child takes, whether she is being weaned from a bottle, going on a first sleep-over, or starting preschool, the child leaves the closeness and total dependence of babyhood behind—a psychological separation from the parent—and may experience feelings of sadness and anger about the loss. However, each child will handle her emotions differently.

When starting school, some children will jump right into the center of the activities and feel comfortable right away; others will need more time to adjust. It is very important to accept your child's own individual reaction.

If this is the first time your child has been apart from you or her babysitter on a regular basis, she may feel anxious about being on her own and act very clingy. Your child may be worrying about many things. Who will take her to the bathroom when she needs to go? Who will zipper her jacket when it's time to play outside? Will you or the babysitter ever come back to get her? You can allay some of her anxiety by reassuring her that the teacher will be there to help her and by keeping her well informed about the daily pickup schedule. Gradually she will learn that the teacher actually does take care of her and that Mommy, Daddy, or her babysitter can leave but they will always come back, and she will calm down.

Your child may cry because she feels sad that you are leaving (a natural reaction to a separation). If so, acknowledge and accept her feelings, support her ability to be independent, and reassure her that you or a designated other person will return for her. You can say, "You're feeling sad. It's hard to say good-bye to Mommy, but you'll manage just fine here and Mommy will pick you up later."

Establishing a good-bye routine with your child, such as having her initiate the "good-bye" hug or wave to you from the window after you leave, can help your child to separate. (She will feel more in control.) Nursery school teachers are very familiar with children's separation reactions and will be there to make suggestions and even cradle a sobbing child.

Some children get angry because they know that the parent will be at home alone with the new baby and they resent being "left at school." If your child seems resentful, you can say, "I see that you are mad about my bringing you here. You are coming here because school is going to be a fun experience for you, and you will learn many new things. You will be fine here."

It often helps to outline the daily tasks that you will be doing at home while your child is at school, such as folding the laundry, going shopping, or cooking dinner, so that your child does not fantasize that you will be sitting and cooing to the baby all morning long.

At home, you can support your child's adjustment by giving her extra attention and reassurance and by making school a part of her home life. Hang up her paintings, display her projects, and talk with her about her experiences. At times, she may not wish to share many details, however, because this is her new private world!

You can help her to deal with her daily challenges by setting up a pretend school for her with her stuffed animals or dolls and acting out ways to cope with the separation, assert herself with a bully, and form friendships. Arranging play dates with her classmates is also extremely beneficial. Once she has one friend to play with at school, she will feel more comfortable.

Before starting school or soon after she begins, your child may revert to some earlier behaviors, such as bed-wetting, thumb sucking, masturbating, clingingness, or uncooperative behavior. This is just a temporary stress reaction and will disappear as soon as she is comfortable in her new environment. Try not to focus on the behavior. Just give your child extra hugs and reassurance and the symptoms will disappear.

Children often complain about going to school long after they are happily adjusted. Your child may begin each morning with "I don't want to go to school" or kick and scream at the classroom door. If you have verified with his teacher that the child is not having any problems at school, this behavior is probably just a form of last-minute protest. If you were to peek into the classroom through a one-way mirror seconds after you departed, you would most likely see your child happily drawing pictures with other children.

Parents often wonder, "Should I persist in sending my four year old to school if she is so sad, angry, wets her bed, and complains every morning?" The answer is yes! Working through her feelings about the separation will help her make a giant leap toward independence, and preschool will enrich her life forever.

Parents Have Separation Anxiety, Too

Parents also have powerful feelings about the separation from their children. Their babies are growing up!

In order to cope best with the situation, try to identify these feelings and allow yourself to experience them (otherwise, you might act them out). If you feel sad about the loss of your "baby" or mad because you need to give her up (or because she is in essence leaving you), it might help to talk with your spouse and other parents about your experience. You will discover that they share the same emotions.

When saying good-bye to your child, it is fine to say, "I'll miss you," but you should convey the same consistent messages to her: "I give you permission to go off and build an independent life, and you can do it."

As a parent, you can comfort yourself by focusing on all the positive experiences that your child will have at school and by keeping in mind that as children grow and separate, we don't lose them. No matter how big your child gets, she will need you forever!

QUESTIONS AND ANSWERS

Our family is moving to a new town. How can we prepare our child?

As soon as it is clear that you will be moving, inform your child and explain to him the reason why (e.g., "We need more room for the family"). Once you have chosen a residence, bring your child to visit. Children adjust best when they have a concrete vision of where they are going. Because a move is a separation, help your child to discuss his sad or angry feelings about leaving his home, his friends, and his school. Help him to build an attachment to his new residence by involving him in choosing some new furnishings or bedding and in meeting some children in the neighborhood. Arrange for a special farewell event and reassure your child that he can call or visit his old friends. In time, your child will adapt to this move because he takes with him the most important ingredient for happiness—he has you!

When we have dinner with our relatives in a restaurant, our daughter insists that we leave the seat next to her for "Griselda," her imaginary companion. We feel embarrassed and are not sure what we should do.

Imaginary friends are companions that children create to keep them company. Your child will invite her imaginary friend to tea, practice the rules with her ("You have to clean up your toys"), and use her to work through her emotions ("Don't be afraid. The monsters won't hurt you"). Be accepting of your child's friend (when she says, "Kiss Griselda goodnight, too," you might go along with it). But when Griselda interferes with family life, set a gentle limit—for example, "We have so many people here tonight that Griselda will have to share your seat!"

Our son makes guns out of everything—a stick, Legos, and even his finger. Should we allow our child to play with toy guns?

Pretend gunplay is a natural part of a child's (especially a boy's) development. When your child wields his stick or points his finger, he feels more powerful in the world. Though the play itself is not harmful, some parents refuse to allow toy guns in their home because of the association with real guns. Others compromise by giving their child a water pistol. Each parent should make his or her own decision. If you decide against them and your child is upset because his best friend has a toy arsenal, you might tell your child, "Toy guns remind us of real guns, and real guns can hurt people. That's why we cannot permit toy guns in our house." It's a hard battle, but stick to your guns!

Should I take my child to her grandmother's funeral?

If your child was close to her grandmother, it might be beneficial for her to go. Attending the funeral would give her a better understanding of what happens to someone when he or she dies. Having the opportunity to participate in saying good-bye to someone she loves and knowing exactly where her grandmother is can help your child with her mourning process. You should explain to your child what will happen at the funeral, suggest that it may be helpful for her to go, and, if feasible, let her decide. If she does agree to attend, prepare her for the possibility that people may be very sad and cry. If you will be occupied, make sure that someone else will be able to sit outside with your child or take her home if she becomes bored or uncomfortable.

Should we allow our four year old to watch television, and if so, how much?

Studies have shown that there are some beneficial effects to television viewing for young children. Children can absorb positive values by watching children's programs that foster prosocial themes, such as sharing, caring, and empathy. They can gain new and exciting information and acquire prereading skills (e.g., letter and word recognition). However, excessive watching limits children's opportunity to learn from real experiences and play (they become passive and less imaginative learners), and violent or scary shows can make children more aggressive and frightened. It is recommended that parents actively guide their child's television viewing by setting limits upon the length of time (one to two hours a day), ruling out violent and frightening shows, and participating whenever possible to monitor and explain the content. (Parents can use the new national rating codes that appear on the television screen and in the television listings to help them determine the age-appropriateness of programs.)

When we catch our son with cookie crumbs all over his face, he tells us he didn't eat any more cookies. What should we do when this happens?

When a small child is caught breaking a rule, he is frightened that you will get angry or punish him, which for him is tantamount to losing your love. Thus, he tries to cover up his misdeed. In a situation when you are sure he has transgressed, confront the misbehavior directly. In this case, you might say, "I see that you have eaten the last two cookies in the jar." Then try not to overreact or call him a liar; otherwise, next time it will be even harder for him to tell you the truth. Simply repeat your rule: "If you want a cookie, you must ask." At a quiet moment, ask him whether he was afraid to tell you the truth because he thought you would get mad. Reinforce the idea that he should always tell you the truth so that you can help him. You might feel angry for a moment, but he cannot lose your love.

The teachers at school are suggesting that we take our daughter for play therapy because she is so aggressive. How can this help?

Your child's aggressive behavior is a symptom that something is bothering her. As your child plays with a doll-house, a board game, or puppets in a relaxed environment, the child therapist will help her to express her feelings and to understand her behavior. The therapist will also meet with you to explain the problem and give you some guidance. In time, the whole family will feel better.

Our child is very active and is not able to sit and focus. Does he have ADHD?

Attention Deficit Hyperactivity Disorder (ADHD) is a neurological problem in which the brain has difficulty filtering irrelevant information and focusing on what is important. Children with this disorder are distracted and impulsive because their attention is being pulled in many different directions at once. (Once the problem is diagnosed, the drug Ritalin [methylphenidate] is often prescribed.) However, distraction, a high activity level, and inattention can be just a part of your child's being a four year old, or a reaction to emotional stress. If you are very concerned, consult with your pediatrician. If an evaluation is recommended, be sure that, besides a neurological exam, the child receives a psychological evaluation from a psychologist to determine whether or not there is an emotional component to his behavior.

Every night our child wants one of us to lie down with him until he falls asleep. We find this extremely exhausting. Is there any way to help him break this habit?

You can change this pattern gradually over several days. If you were lying on the bed with him, move to a chair the first night. The next night, move the chair a few feet away from the bed. Then, slowly but surely, introduce some brief absences to help him build up his tolerance. You might say, "I'll be right back. I have to go to the kitchen for a moment." Eventually you can set a timer and tell him that you are going out and will return to tuck him in when the timer goes off, in ten minutes.

Recently, I have begun to make frequent business trips. How can I help my child adjust to my absences?

It is helpful to explain to your child exactly what you do at work (if possible, have her visit you) and why you need to travel sometimes. Reassure her that you miss her very much when you are away. Before a trip, you might mark off on a calendar the number of days you will be away, and pinpoint your destination on a map or a globe for her. To ease the separation when you are away, call her each day (if you can), send her picture postcards (she can collect them), leave her a small gift for each day you will be away, or have her listen to a tape recording of you reading her favorite story, at bedtime.

GLOSSARY

Aggressive impulses sudden, spontaneous hostile urges.

Attention Deficit Hyperactivity Disorder (ADHD) a difficulty in maintaining a focus of attention.

Child development specialist someone who has had professional training in early childhood development, including a mental health professional, a teacher, a physician, or a nurse.

Counseling (often referred to as psychotherapy) a process by which a professional helps individuals, couples, and families to talk about and resolve emotional issues.

Egocentric thinking, observing, or judging things in relation to the self.

Empathy the ability to place oneself in another person's shoes and comprehend his or her thoughts or feelings.

Mental health professional (often referred to as a counselor or a psychotherapist) a social worker, psychologist, psychiatrist, or counselor who is trained to advise and counsel individuals.

Mourning process the process through which individuals grieve a death or any other loss.

Play therapy a form of counseling that is done with children through play.

Regress to return to a behavior related to an earlier developmental stage.

Repress to hide from conscious thought ideas and feelings that are thought to be unacceptable.

Self-esteem an individual's sense of his own worth.

Separation anxiety the emotional reaction to a physical or psychological separation, which usually includes feelings of sadness and anger.

Separation the process whereby the child achieves a psychological independence from her parent and becomes more of an independent person.

Temperament the individual's unique way of responding to the environment.

SUGGESTED READING

FOR ADULTS

Balaban, N., *Starting School.* New York: Teachers College Press, 1985.

Ferber, R., M.D., *Solve Your Child's Sleep Problems.* New York: Simon & Schuster, 1985.

Fraiberg, S., *The Magic Years.* New York: Charles Scribner's Sons, 1959.

Galinsky, E., & David, J., *The Preschool Years.* New York: Ballantine Books, 1988.

Ginott, H., *Between Parent and Child.* New York: Avon Books, 1956.

Goleman, D., *Emotional Intelligence.* New York: Bantam Books, 1995.

Gottlieb, S., *Keys to Children's Sleep Problems.* Hauppauge, N.Y.: Barron's Educational Series, Inc., 1993.

Grollman, E., *Talking About Death.* Boston: Beacon Press, 1990.

Kubler-Ross, E., *On Death and Dying.* New York: Macmillan, 1969.

Samalin, N., *Loving Your Child Is Not Enough.* New York: Penguin Books, 1987.

Siegel, E., & Seigel, L., *Keys to Disciplining Your Young Child*. Hauppauge, N.Y.: Barron's Educational Series, Inc., 1993.

Talking About Child Sexual Abuse (a pamphlet for parents). Published by National Committee for the Prevention of Child Abuse, (312) 663-3520.

Turecki, S., *The Difficult Child*. New York: Bantam Books, 1985.

FOR CHILDREN

Explaining Birth/The New Baby

Andry, A., & Schepp, S., *How Babies Are Made*. Boston: Little, Brown & Company, 1968.

Cole, J., *How You Were Born*. New York: Morrow Junior Books, 1993.

Cole, J., *The New Baby at Your House*. New York: William Morrow & Company, Inc., 1985.

Horowitz, R., *Mommy's Lap*. New York: Lothrop, Lee & Shepard Books, 1993.

Rogers, F., *The New Baby*. New York: G. P. Putnam's Sons, 1985.

Explaining Death

Mellonie, B., & Ingpen, R., *Lifetimes*. New York: Bantam Books, 1983.

Rogers, F., *When a Pet Dies*. New York: G. P. Putnam's Sons, 1988.

Viorst, J., *The Tenth Good Thing About Barney*. New York: Aladdin Books, 1971.

Divorce and Stepfamily Relationships

Best, C., *Getting Used to Harry*. New York: Orchard Books, 1996.

Brown, L. K., & Brown, M., *Dinosaurs Divorce*. New York: Little, Brown & Company, 1986.

Rogers, F., *Let's Talk About It: Divorce*. New York: G. P. Putnam's Sons, 1996.

Sinberg, J., *Divorce Is a Grown Up Problem*. New York: Avon, 1978.

Safety and Strangers

Berenstain, S. & J., *Berenstain Bears Learn About Strangers*. New York: Random House, 1985.

Walvoord Girard, L., *My Body Is Private*. Morton Grove, Ind.: Albert Whitman & Co., 1984.

Miscellaneous

Crary, E., *I'm Mad*. Seattle: Parenting Press, Inc., 1992.

Feller, C., *My Mom Travels a Lot*. New York: Puffin Books, 1981.

Hoban, R., *Bedtime for Frances*. New York: HarperCollins Publishers, 1960.

Kasza, K., *A Mother for Chocho* (adoption). New York: The Putnam & Grosset Group, 1992.

Kuklin, S., *Going to My Nursery School*. New York: Bradbury Press, 1990.

Mayle, P. *What's Happening to Me?* (physical development). New York: First Carol Publishing Group, 1989.

Rogers, F., *Moving*. New York: G. P. Putnam's Sons, 1987.

RESOURCES

American Psychological Association (APA)
1200 17th Street NW
Washington, DC 20009
(800) 374-2721

American Speech-Language-Hearing Association
10801 Rockville Pike
Rockville, MD 20852
(800) 638-8255
(Brochures available on hearing and speech topics)

ChildHelp (National Child Abuse Hotline)
(800) 422-4453
(24-hour resource and referral for parents under stress)

**Children and Adults with Attention Deficit Disorder
(CHADD)**
499 Northwest 70th Street
Suite 308
Plantation, FL 33317
(305) 587-3700

**National Association for the Education of
Young Children (NAEYC)**
1834 Connecticut Avenue NW
Washington, DC 20009
(800) 424-2460

National Association of Social Workers (NASW)
7981 Eastern Avenue
Silver Springs, MD 20910
(800) 227-3590

**National Information Center for Children and Youths
with Handicaps (NICHCY)**
PO Box 1492
Washington, DC 20012
(703) 893-6061

**National Institute for Mental Health, Alcohol, Drug
Abuse, and Mental Health Administration**
Park Lawn Building, 15C-05
5600 Fishers Lane
Rockville, MD 20857
(301) 443-4513

INDEX